Elite • 211

The SAS 1983–2014

LEIGH NEVILLE

ILLUSTRATED BY PETER DENNIS
Series editor Martin Windrow

First published in Great Britain in 2016 by Osprey Publishing
PO Box 883, Oxford, OX1 9PL, UK
1385 Broadway, 5th Floor, New York, NY 10018, USA.
E-mail: info@ospreypublishing.com

Osprey Publishing, part of Bloomsbury Publishing Plc

A CIP catalogue record for this book is available from the British Library

Print ISBN: 978 1 47281 403 6
PDF ebook ISBN: 978 1 47281 404 3
ePub ebook ISBN: 978 1 47281 405 0

Editor: Martin Windrow
Index by Rob Munro
Typeset in Sabon and Myriad Pro
Originated by PDQ Media, Bungay, UK
Printed in China through Worldprint Ltd

16 17 18 19 20 10 9 8 7 6 5 4 3 2 1

Osprey Publishing supports the Woodland Trust, the UK's leading woodland conservation charity. Between 2014 and 2018 our donations will be spent on their Centenary Woods project in the UK.

www.ospreypublishing.com

TITLE PAGE Member of an unidentified UKSF unit in a Menacity SRV/OAV during a halt in Afghanistan, muffled against the winter cold of the high desert. The L7A2 GPMG is on a WMIK-style swing-out MG mount, and a sand channel to assist in extracting bogged vehicles is attached to the front grille.

BACK COVER, TOP An SAS operator in southern Iraq, c.2007, wearing a temperate-pattern DPM smock with desert-pattern trousers – a combination more commonly seen in Afghanistan. His weapon is a CQB-barrel 'shorty' L119A1 carbine. The obscuring of his face hides his MSA Sordins headset, but a CT5 handset is attached to his plate carrier at the left shoulder. Note the fast-roping gloves tucked behind a magazine pouch.

DEDICATION

To the Regiment

We are the Pilgrims, master; we shall go

Always a little further: it may be

Beyond that last blue mountain barred with snow,

Across that angry or that glimmering sea.

(From James Elroy Flecker, 'The Golden Journey to Samarkand')

ACKNOWLEDGEMENTS & AUTHOR'S NOTE

My thanks to my editor Martin Windrow, and our wonderful illustrator Peter Dennis; to my wife Jodi; and to the many who have provided information or views during the research for this book.

The aim of this work is to provide an update on the Regiment since the end of Operation 'Corporate' in the South Atlantic in 1982, which is deliberately excluded here as it has potential for its own standalone title. We begin our coverage nominally from 1983, when the Regiment was still bathed in the bright spotlight of unwanted publicity due to their exploits both at the Iranian Embassy siege in London in 1980 and in the Falklands two years later.

As well as being one of the most widely recognized special forces units in the world, the SAS are also one of the tightest-lipped. After a rash of memoirs following Operation 'Granby' in 1991, the Regiment instituted lifelong non-disclosure agreements with all badged members and support staff. This publicity-shy attitude means that there are quite literally no official images of SAS operations or training available, nor are former operators able to be interviewed openly.

In all the images used here the faces have, of course, been obscured, as have some other sensitive details; we believe that, if anything, we have erred on the side of caution. Many of the photos were taken during deployments, and most cannot be attributed to an individual; unless specifically credited otherwise the photographer is unknown. If you believe that you hold the copyright to any such image, please contact the author via Osprey Publishing, and we will happily issue corrections in future editions.

ARTIST'S NOTE

Initial abbreviations used in this text

ASU	Active Service Unit (of the PIRA)
CQB	Close-quarter battle
COIN	Counter-insurgency (covers all relevant techniques, based on enlisting the support of local populations as well as 'direct action')
CT	Counter-terrorist
DPV	Desert Patrol Vehicle
EOD	Explosive Ordnance Disposal ('bomb disposal')
HALO	High Altitude, Low Opening (parachute insertion technique; equally, HAHO: 'high opening')
IED	Improvised explosive device
ISTAR	Intelligence, Surveillance, Target Acquisition & Reconnaissance
JSOC	Joint Special Operations Command (American)
MoD	Ministry of Defence (British)
PIRA	Provisional Irish Republican Army (terrorist group)
ROE	Rules of engagement
RSM	Regimental Sergeant Major
SAM	Surface-to-air missile
SAS	Special Air Service (British regiment)
SASR	Special Air Service Regiment (Australian)
SBS	Special Boat Service
SFSG	Special Forces Support Group
SIS	Secret Intelligence Service (aka MI6)
SOF	Special operations forces (generic term)
SP	Special Projects (22 SAS CT Team)
SRR	Special Reconnaissance Regiment
SRV/OAV	Surveillance & Reconnaissance Vehicle/Offensive Action Vehicle
UAV	Unmanned aerial vehicle ('drone')
UKSF	United Kingdom Special Forces
WMIK	Weapon Mounted Installation Kit (i.e armed Land Rover)

CONTENTS

THE SPECIAL AIR SERVICE 1983–2014

INTRODUCTION: THE PILGRIMS

The Special Air Service (SAS) should need little introduction, since they are arguably the most recognized, and certainly the most emulated, Special Forces unit in the world today. Their history is equally legendary. Formed in 1941 by a visionary Scots Guards officer named David Stirling, the SAS soon developed a fearsome reputation while working alongside the Long Range Desert Group to raid Axis airfields and supply dumps in North Africa. Expanded, it went on to carry out deep-penetration missions in Italy and North-West Europe in 1943–45. Like many other World War II special operations units, the original SAS was disbanded after the end of hostilities in 1945.

Recognizing the need for such a unit in the new Cold War era of proxy wars, Britain raised one Regular Army and two Territorial Army SAS regiments in the 1950s. These would be known, respectively, as 22 SAS, 21 SAS (Artists Rifles) and 23 SAS, the latter two forming the core of the UK Special Forces Reserve until 2014.[1] During the Cold War the SAS would serve in a number of counter-insurgency (COIN) and counter-terrorist (CT) campaigns in Malaya, Borneo, Oman, Aden, Gambia, and Northern Ireland. In many of these conflicts the SAS operated covertly, and their presence was often not acknowledged at the time. Their unique skills would also enable them to form the UK's national CT response, a role they continue to fulfil to this day.

In 1982, elements of 22 SAS deployed to the South Atlantic in support of Operation 'Corporate', the liberation of the Falkland Islands after the Argentine invasion of that April. Due to a tragic crash involving a Sea King helicopter, this deployment resulted in the Regiment's highest number of casualties since World War II. Their most public success was the raid on Pebble Island on 14/15 May, which crippled much of the Argentine Air Force's ground-attack capability in an operation that echoed the unit's wartime exploits in North Africa.

Organization

22 SAS is known colloquially as 'the Regiment'. It is organized into a number of 'sabre squadrons' – the terminology dates back to their earliest days, when

---

1 In that year both 21 and 23 SAS were placed under the command of the newly raised 1st Intelligence, Surveillance & Reconnaissance (ISR) Brigade. Both regiments now have a new role conducting Human Environment Reconnaissance & Analysis (HERA) patrols in conflict areas, in support of broader ISR objectives.

Although no images are available of the British SAS Special Projects Team's current dress, this Australian image from 2006 should be indicative of their equipment. It shows an Australian Special Air Service Regiment (SASR) counter-terrorism operator from Tactical Assault Group-East dressed in full 'black kit', and carrying both a 9x19mm MP5 sub-machine gun and a 9x19mm USP pistol. Note the Rabintex RBH Attack ballistic helmet with mount for night-vision goggles. (Courtesy LAC Rodney Welch, Australian Defense Force)

the unit's name was intended to confuse German intelligence. One squadron is maintained on CT duty in the UK; a second will probably be on a deployment (to Afghanistan, for example); a third will be preparing for deployment whilst conducting short-term training; and the fourth will be on longer-term overseas training, such as jungle or desert exercises. Of course, in times of war such as the invasion of Iraq in 2003, it is not unusual for two squadrons to deploy for operations (indeed, during Operation 'Granby' in 1990–91 the best part of three squadrons deployed to Saudi Arabia).

Each 'squadron' typically comprises four 'troops', each composed of some 16 soldiers and specializing in a particular insertion method – Air, Boat, Mountain, and Mobility – although all SAS soldiers are expected to be proficient in each (for instance, all are parachute- and most are HALO-qualified). Each SAS soldier – variously known as a 'blade' or 'operator' – is also trained in one particular core skill, as a medic, demolitions man, linguist or signaller (radio operator). British SAS patrols are typically four-man (Australian Special Air Service Regiment (SASR) patrols are usually five strong), although the structure is intended to allow great flexibility; many SAS force elements are formed from two or more patrols, depending upon the task.

Those wishing to serve in this most elite of units must pass a gruelling evaluation programme known simply as UKSF Selection, including the infamous Survive, Evade, Resist and Extract (SERE) Phase, during which members of the Special Forces Support Group (SFSG) act as a hunter force and the candidates are the hunted. Selection is a six-month process which tests candidates physically, mentally and emotionally to ascertain whether they have the right combination of qualities for the Regiment. Although many of the candidates are already the best that the regular Army can offer, fewer than 10 per cent of them complete Selection and go on to be 'badged', earning the right to wear the famous sand-colour beret.

OPERATIONS:

SPECIAL PROJECTS
'London Bridge' was the innocuous code word to launch the assault on the Iranian Embassy in Prince's Gate, London on 5 May 1980, provoked by the confirmed murder of one of the 20 hostages. Deployed following the seizure

UNIFORMS & EQUIPMENT (I)
1: Ulster Troop, 22 SAS; Intelligence & Security Group, Northern Ireland, 1986
Representing an undercover operator deployed to the Province, this figure sports the classic 1980s SAS undercover look of 'bomber jacket', blue jeans, suede desert boots, 'unmilitary' hair and a big, droopy moustache. The SAS contingent were not considered to be terribly adept at 'merging with the population', since apart from the haircut this look was characteristic of most off-duty soldiers. He carries the then recently issued Heckler & Koch G3K rifle in 7.62x51mm NATO; it was preferred over the Regiment's earlier MP5s and HK53s due to its penetrative capabilities, particularly when engaging targets in or behind cars – a common occurrence in SAS ambushes.

2: B Squadron, 22 SAS; Western Iraq, 1991
A member of one of the reconnaissance patrols tasked with establishing observation posts (OPs) on the Main Supply Routes (MSRs), he wears a relatively rare patrol cap in desert Disruptive Pattern Material (DPM); a hooded desert windproof smock dating back to the birth of the SAS (and, incredibly, still held in Quartermaster stores ready for issue some 50 years later); and standard issue desert-pattern DPM combat trousers. His load-bearing chest rig is a commercial design from Arktis, although many wore hand-painted and modified versions of the issue Personal Load-Carrying Equipment (PLCE) assault vest, or privately purchased South African Defence Force M83 vests. He carries an L108A1 Minimi light machine gun, a weapon adopted by the SAS a good decade

before the British Army adopted the shorter-barrel L110A2 Para version as an Urgent Operational Requirement for Afghanistan.
Hidden about his person in a concealed money belt would be 20 gold sovereigns, and a reward note in both Arabic and English promising £50,000 to the recipient if they helped the operator to the nearest British embassy or consulate. The teams also carried silk escape maps. Each operator was given a cover story that they were a security element for a Search-and-Rescue unit whose helicopter had been shot down; they were under strict orders to maintain the deception for at least 24 hours, to allow any potentially compromised codes and callsigns to be changed.

3: D Squadron, 22 SAS; Saudi Arabia, 1990
This operator is portrayed as if training for the (thankfully aborted) hostage rescue of some 800 Western, Japanese and Kuwaiti civilians being held by the Iraqi invaders of Kuwait as 'human shields'. He wears a mix of standard CT 'black kit' and issue uniform items; the desert DPM pattern is the earlier, sparser version that was pinker in tone. His vest is the Armourshield REV25 (Restricted Entry Vest), which could be upgraded with ballistic trauma plates to increase protection levels. His weapons are the standard 9x19mm Heckler & Koch MP5A3 and a Browning pistol in a leather drop holster on his right thigh. On an actual operation he would also wear an assault vest carrying extra magazines, G60 'flashbang' grenades, a rescue knife and plastic restraints. His balaclava would also probably be replaced with a Nomex anti-flash hood, and an S10 respirator if CS gas was to be deployed.

An Australian Tactical Assault Group dismount from a modified Toyota Land Cruiser as they storm a simulated terrorist stronghold (note the extended running boards and grab handles, along with a roof-mounted ladder platform; assaulters ride the vehicle into the target). The operators carry a mix of MP5s and M4A5 carbines depending on role. The pink fragments on the ground in the right foreground are from an exploded watermelon; representing a terrorist sentry for the purposes of this exercise, it was hit moments earlier by a sniper team. (Courtesy LAC Rodney Welch, Australian Defense Force)

An Australian SASR counter-terrorist team photographed in 2003. The operators carry a mix of MP5 models including the A5, SD3 and KA1; all have Aimpoint optics mounted 'high' for use when wearing respirators, which reduce vision. (Courtesy LAC Rodney Welch, Australian Defense Force)

of the Embassy by Iranian terrorists on 30 April, some 44 members of the Regiment's B Sqn, supported by an additional six snipers on the outer cordon, stormed the Embassy. That day a contemporary military legend was born, as Operation 'Nimrod' made the SAS a household name. Many readers of a certain age will still remember the televised final of the World Snooker Championships being interrupted by a live outside broadcast from the Embassy. Black-clad figures could be seen swarming over the balconies at the front of the building before detonating frame charges to blow in the reinforced-glass doors. Moments later they disappeared inside, with their progress marked thereafter by the sounds of automatic weapons fire and the dull thump of 'flashbang' grenades.

The SAS had been given responsibility for providing the British Army's CT response several days after the tragic events at the Munich Olympic Games on 5–6 September 1972. In a little over a month the first 20-man SAS CT unit was ready to respond to similar incidents within the United Kingdom or abroad. Known variously as the Pagoda Team (after Operation 'Pagoda', the codename for the development of the SAS CT capability), the SP or Special Projects Team, or the Anti-Terrorist Team, this was initially composed of members from all squadrons, particularly from those who had experience in the Regiment's Bodyguarding Cell, which taught close-quarter battle (CQB) with pistols.

SAS operators conducting training with the MP5A3 at the Pontrilas Army Training Area, c. 2004.

The fledgling unit was soon placed under the control of the Regiment's Counter Revolutionary Warfare Wing – a then-recent innovation that initially consisted of a single SAS officer tasked with monitoring terrorism developments, but which was soon expanded – and was trimmed in size to single-troop strength. These soldiers were equipped with standard Browning pistols, Ingram Model 10 sub-machine guns (soon to be replaced with the Heckler & Koch MP5), Remington shotguns for blowing off locks, and black Nomex flight suits. British technical experts developed a number of innovations for the team, including the first experimental 'flashbang' or 'stun' grenade, and one of the earliest examples of frangible ammunition that would reduce the risk of over-penetration in situations involving hostages.

The Regiment's first known home operation in this role was something of an anti-climax, when on 7 January 1975 a hijacked British Airways BAC One-Eleven landed at Stansted Airport in Essex. The hijacker, an Iranian armed with a replica pistol, was captured alive with no shots fired, and the only casualty was an SAS soldier who was bitten by a police dog as he left the airliner.

Eventually the CT unit would grow to full squadron strength, and included its own support elements – Explosive Ordnance Disposal (EOD), search and combat dogs, medics, and an attached intelligence and targeting cell. The CT role was shared amongst the squadrons on a 12-month and later six-month rotation basis, to ensure that all members were eventually trained in CT and CQB techniques. (Today, all candidates for the SAS and SBS on UKSF Selection undertake a three-week CT course as part of the selection process, thus ensuring that all members understand at least the basic concepts of CT direct action.)

Overseas co-operation

Counter-terrorism became something of a growth industry for the SAS in the 1980s. Every nation friendly to Britain (and some not so friendly) wanted a CT capability just like the Special Air Service. The Ministry of Defence (MoD) and the Foreign & Commonwealth Office had for many years loaned out training teams from the Regiment, particularly to the Gulf States, to train bodyguard teams; now those training packages turned their hand to counter-terrorism.

The Regiment also began a long-standing association with their American counterparts in the 1st Special Forces Operational Detachment-Delta (more commonly known as Delta Force, or by its cover name, the Combat

An American 'Shoot House', better known in the SAS as a 'Killing House'. During live hostage-survival training senior politicians and members of the royal family have sat inside the Regiment's version of this facility, while live rounds cracked past and 'flashbangs' exploded around them. One of the most famous drills (and the most terrifying for the mock hostages) is for the SP Team to conduct an entry in complete darkness using their night-vision goggles. (Courtesy Sgt Steven L. Phillips, US Army)

Applications Group). The two units swapped techniques and equipment and conducted joint exercises in both America and Europe. Other nations' CT units also developed close ties with the Regiment, including the German GSG9, the French GIGN, and the New Zealand and Australian SAS units. (SAS personnel had accompanied GSG9 during their rescue of 86 hostages held on the hijacked Lufthansa Flight 181 Boeing 737 in Mogadishu, Somalia on 18 October 1977, and had supplied early examples of their 'stun' grenades to create a diversion as the GSG9 assault went in.)

During the late 1980s members of the Regiment were dispatched to train Colombian special operations forces in counter-terrorism and counter-narcotics operations. In common with many SAS training-team missions this remains shrouded in secrecy; there have been whispers of SAS operators, like their US counterparts, accompanying Colombian elements on jungle operations, but this is never likely to be confirmed.[2]

Along with the overseas training missions, the Regiment would send small teams to act as observers, and to provide advice or technical input if required, at the scenes of terrorist and similar incidents worldwide. These included such far-flung locations as the siege at Waco, Texas in 1993, where both Delta and SAS observers were deployed; the rescue by GIGN of hostages held on an Air France A300 airliner in Marseille in 1994; and the Japanese Embassy siege in Lima, Peru in 1996.

Home operations

The Regiment also assisted authorities a little closer to home in what would become another of their rare officially acknowledged CT deployments on UK soil. At Peterhead Prison in Scotland a number of rioting inmates took a prison officer hostage in October 1987. With the prisoners and their hostage barricaded, the Prison Service and police lacked the necessary explosive

---

2 Indeed, A Sqn were returning from a Colombian deployment in August 1990 when Iraq invaded Kuwait. This led to an unseemly squabble over whether A or G Sqn – who were on SP rotation, but had just returned from a stint of desert training, and thus were the more logical choice – would be deployed to the Gulf. Since A Sqn had 'missed out' on the Falklands, they eventually got the nod.

breaching skills to facilitate a hostage rescue, so military assistance was requested. D Squadron, the on-call CT rotation at the time, was notified, and a small element was flown up to the prison. Wearing their trademark 'black kit' and carrying batons along with their Browning pistols as last-ditch personal protection, the SAS conducted multiple coordinated explosive breaches, deploying both CS gas grenades and 'flashbangs' as they entered. The hostage-takers were immediately overwhelmed, and the prison officer was rescued and carried to safety through a hole made in the roof. The Regiment left as quickly and as quietly as they had arrived. In all, the actual hostage rescue had lasted just six minutes, without a shot being fired.

Into the 1990s the operational pace hardly slackened for the CT rotation, although (aside from reinforcement and support to the Ulster-based SAS troop – see below) they were rarely deployed on live operations within the United Kingdom. Techniques were constantly enhanced and learning was shared between international CT units, with the SAS developing aerial sniping, vehicle interdiction using Hatton shotgun shells, and a number of innovative non-explosive methods of entry. Many of these techniques would first see operational use a number of years later on the new battlefields of Afghanistan and Iraq. Tactics for home deployments in support of police were also developed, in two stages. The Immediate Action (IA) plan is put into effect as soon as the Regiment arrives at the location of the incident; it is a rough-and-ready concept, in case the terrorists start killing hostages and immediate SAS intervention is required. As time progresses the IA plan is improved upon, to increase the chances of success and reduce the risk of 'friendly' casualties. A separate Deliberate Action (DA) plan is developed in parallel. This is essentially the full 'bells and whistles' plan that is reckoned to have the best chance of success; it is based on a timescale and entry points of the Regiment's choosing.

On 6 February 2000, a Boeing 727 airliner operated by Ariana (Afghanistan's national carrier at the time) was hijacked by a number of Afghan nationals who wished to escape the country and to obtain the release of a *mujahideen* warlord imprisoned by the Taliban. The flight eventually landed in the UK at Stansted Airport, with the on-call CT Team racing down from Hereford. Upon deployment the team linked up with the armed police containment, and began to develop both its IA and DA plans; neither were eventually required, as the hijackers surrendered.

The SAS train for the CT role at the Pontrilas Army Training Area in a facility that includes a recently rebuilt 'Killing House' (officially known as the 'Close Quarter Battle House'), with moveable rubber furniture and walls to replicate any target location. Part of a Boeing 747 airliner can also be reconfigured to match the internal layouts of virtually any commercial aircraft. The on-call CT squadron is split into four troops, two of which are on immediate notice to move and are restricted to the Hereford-Credenhill area, while the other pair conduct training and exercises across the UK but are available for operational deployment should the need arise, for example in response to multiple terrorist incidents.

July 2005, and since

After the events of 7 July 2005, when four terrorist suicide bombers murdered 52 civilians and wounded some 700 in three London underground trains and a bus (followed by an abortive attempt to repeat this atrocity on 21 July), a small forward element from the SP Team was permanently deployed to the nation's capital to provide immediate assistance to the Metropolitan Police in the event of a terrorist incident. This unit is supported by its own attached Ammunition Technical Officers (ATOs) trained in high-risk search and making safe car bombs and improvised explosive devices (IEDs), along with a technical intelligence cell capable of sophisticated interception of all forms of communication.

The police retain primacy and are the lead agency in the event of a terrorist act on UK soil. The military will provide support as requested, including by UK Special Forces. If a situation is deemed to be outside the capabilities of police firearms units (for instance, if it requires specialist breaching capabilities), the SAS will be called in under the Military Aid to the Civil Authorities (MACA) legislation. Additionally, some categories of operation – such as the recapture of hijacked airliners or cruise ships, or the recovery of nuclear or radioactive IEDs – remain a military responsibility.

In the aftermath of the attempted bombings on 21 July 2005, several SAS elements trained in explosive methods of entry (E-MOE) were dispatched to support the Metropolitan Police firearms unit. The operators were armed only with sidearms for self-defence, and were used only to explosively breach into two flats where the would-be bombers had taken refuge. The police firearms teams fired CS gas into both premises and negotiated the surrender of all suspects. There was no further known SAS involvement. Support was also provided by the then newly formed Special Reconnaissance Regiment (SRR), who attached an unarmed member to each of the Met's surveillance teams to provide additional capability to a seriously stretched SO12 (the former name for the Met's surveillance unit).

ULSTER

Although the Regiment had been deployed to Northern Ireland in support of Operation 'Banner' since 1976, when D Sqn first deployed overtly, it was during the 1980s that they built for themselves an almost mythical reputation. Wanted Provisional Irish Republican Army (PIRA) terrorists were snatched

B

UNIFORMS & EQUIPMENT (II)

1: D Squadron, 22 SAS; Operation 'Barras', Sierra Leone, 2000

He wears issue Combat 95 temperate-pattern DPM uniform, with Adidas GSG9 boots and, unusually for the time, an issue Mk 6 helmet complete with scrim netting and 'para tape'. Before Operation 'Telic' in Iraq in 2003 helmets were still rarely worn on SAS operations; many argued that they impeded hearing and presented a more obvious target, as well as being hot and heavy. He carries a 5.56x45mm M16A1 assault rifle fitted with a 40mm M203 underslung grenade-launcher.

2: A Squadron, 22 SAS; Operation 'Trent', Afghanistan, 2001

This operator wears an SAS smock in temperate DPM with desert DPM combat trousers; note also the single Blackhawk Industries knee pad, showing the custom of wearing the pad only on the knee used to support a kneeling firing position. His helmet is the American MSA MICH TC-2000, with a field-expedient desert DPM cover. His body armour is the Blackhawk Industries STRIKE plate carrier in black. Plate carriers offer less protection, but, being smaller and lighter than more conventional body armour, they are often preferred by special operators. Over it, to carry his magazines and grenades, he wears an olive-drab Eagle chest rig. His weapon is the L119A1 fitted with an Advanced Combat Optical Gunsight (ACOG) and a 40mm Heckler & Koch AG-C L17A1 underslung grenade-launcher.

3: Task Force Black/Task Force Knight, 22 SAS; Iraq, 2005

An American-issue Army Combat Uniform (ACU) pattern combat shirt is worn here with American Desert Camouflage Uniform (DCU) trousers. The helmet is a Gentex, with a Selex Assault 700 headset underneath to allow uninhibited communications with fellow assaulters on the objective. His plate carrier is the MSA Paraclete Releasable Assault Vest (RAV) with a mix of Blackhawk Industries pouches, including for his Cougar Racal and CT5 handset; a Petzl headlamp is visible attached directly to the vest beside the pistol holster. Note also the coloured Union flag patch, with a very unofficial 'F**k al Qaeda' upper motto, on the front of his Paraclete vest. The tan Oakley assault gloves eventually became an Afghan-specific issue for the British Army as a whole. He carries both a suppressed and accessorized L119A1, and, hanging from a bungee cord, a sawn-off L74A1 shotgun for breaching, with ammo in attached 'Side Saddles'.

These snipers in a helicopter carry G3K rifles, as favoured by the SAS in Northern Ireland, but here equipped for a very different role. This is an example of aerial sniping overwatch during a CT exercise in the UK; in the background, operators fast-rope from the Sea King helicopter onto the deck of a Royal Navy vessel. (Courtesy UK MoD)

from their homes across the border in the Republic, and Active Service Units (ASUs) were ambushed and shot down as they approached weapons caches by men in unmarked uniforms or civilian dress, carrying non-standard weapons. The SAS's early successes led to increasing paranoia within Republican circles, as the PIRA hunted for the informers they felt certain must be in their midst.

The Regiment had increased their operational focus on Northern Ireland, with a small element known as the Ulster Troop or simply 'the Troop' permanently stationed in the province to provide specialist support to the Army and the Royal Ulster Constabulary (RUC). This troop consisted of around 20 operators and associated support personnel, serving on a rotational basis. For larger pre-planned operations, this Ulster Troop was reinforced directly from Hereford with additional SAS soldiers, often in small packets of two to three men drawn from the on-call Special Projects Team.

From 1980, the Troop served 12-month tours instead of the earlier six-month rotations, as it was felt that longer deployments allowed the operators to develop and maintain a better understanding of the key factions and players. Surveillance was an important aspect of the Troop's remit; the Army Surveillance Unit, later known as 14 Intelligence & Security Company (and more commonly as 'the Det') also often conducted surveillance operations that led to SAS ambushes. Both organizations reported to an Army command known as the Intelligence & Security Group or 'the Group'.

OP/React – shoot to kill?

The SAS conducted a large number of what were officially called 'OP/React' operations – reactive observation posts or, more bluntly, ambushes – acting on information provided from a range of sources including informers and technical intelligence. The Det, the Secret Intelligence Service (SIS, aka 'MI6') and the RUC's E4A surveillance unit would target ASU members, tracking them until a terrorist operation was thought to be imminent. At that point the SAS were handed control, and would plan an arrest operation. Such operations would see a patrol from the resident Troop establish a covert watch over a PIRA arms or explosives cache. When the terrorists arrived to either hide or recover weapons, they were challenged by the operators. If the terrorists were armed and did not instantly comply with the challenge, they were engaged.

A plain-clothes SAS operator, during a much more recent and sunnier deployment than Ulster, carrying a CQB-barrel L119A1 fitted with a light mount and ACOG optical sight. In Northern Ireland the even shorter MP5K was a weapon of choice for operators in surveillance cars, who often travelled with one such weapon hidden in the footwell.

One example of such an operation was the ambush of three ASU members in Strabane in February 1985. An ASU was tasked with attacking an RUC Land Rover with homemade anti-tank grenades, and visited a weapons cache to hide the grenades after a fruitless hunt for a suitable target. Unbeknown to them, three SAS operators were lying in wait in a covert observation post (OP) at the cache site, and a fourth was stationed at a nearby Security Forces base acting as a liaison with the local Army unit. As the terrorists approached the cache, weapons in hand, they were fired upon by the trio of SAS operators, killing all three in a confused engagement before they managed to get a shot off. It seemed the perfect operation – identified armed terrorists intercepted and eliminated – but it led to some awkward questions for the Regiment. According to the inquest, the SAS operators fired a total of 117 rounds, of which 28 struck one ASU member alone. Most intriguingly, two of the operators had engaged the terrorists with their 9mm Browning High-Power pistols, both claiming that they had suffered stoppages with their HK53 carbines. The inquest also found that the balaclavas the ASU wore showed no bullet holes, although all three men had gunshot wounds to the head, leading to speculation that the operators had engaged them with their HK53s and then finished them off with their pistols after removing the balaclavas to confirm identities.

Other operations saw ASUs intercepted on their way to or at the sites of planned attacks, such as the December 1984 ambush of two terrorists who attempted to assassinate a reserve soldier outside the hospital where he worked. Instead they were intercepted by an SAS team who were shadowing them in a number of undercover cars, and both were shot dead as they approached their intended victim.

There was considerable speculation in the media over the years concerning allegations of a so-called 'shoot-to-kill' policy by the Regiment. These allegations tended to focus on whether a terrorist could have been captured alive rather than killed. Certainly, after the 1980 murder of SAS Capt Herbert Westmacott (killed after terrorists waved a white flag), and the death in December 1984 of an SAS lance-corporal, members of the Regiment appear to have adopted an unofficial policy of what military historian Mark Urban quoted SAS sources as calling 'Big boys' games – big boys' rules': simply put, if you're an armed terrorist you can expect no quarter to be given. (After all, the PIRA themselves never took prisoners except with the very worst of intentions.)

Despite this, notes from SAS Order Groups at the time specifically mention 'apprehending suspects' rather than anything more explicitly lethal.[3] The SAS are intensively trained to continue firing until their target is on the ground, no longer moving and no longer a threat. For instance, during the Iranian Embassy operation a number of the terrorists were shot anywhere between 15 and 39 times. Also according to SAS sources, only a quarter of SAS operations in Northern Ireland ended in shooting; the vast majority successfully apprehended their quarry without a shot being fired. As an example, the SAS captured alive an ASU who had been firing a .50cal Barrett sniper rifle from within the modified boot (trunk) of a Mazda 332 sedan; at the time of the SAS operation, the sniper cell was one of a pair responsible for the deaths of nine members of the security forces. Such restraint argues a high level of discipline.

An SAS ambush in May 1987 known as Operation 'Judy', outside the village of Loughgall, resulted in the largest loss of ASU members in the PIRA's history, when eight armed terrorists were shot and killed as they attempted to blow up a police station using a 90kg explosive device carried in the bucket of a mechanical digger. The PIRA plan was to breach the station's perimeter fence with the digger before detonating the device to blow up the building. A stolen Toyota Hiace van would be used to transport the other ASU members to and from the target. A number of RUC officers and seven SAS soldiers were stationed within the police station to deceive the terrorists into thinking that the evacuated station was still fully manned. Outside, an SAS ambush party of more than 30 operators waited in concealed positions; the resident SAS troop had been reinforced by a further 15 operators from G Sqn who were flown in from Hereford specifically for the operation. The ambush team were well armed with a pair of light-role L7A2 General Purpose Machine Guns (GPMGs), and individual operators carried a mixture of M16s and the newly issued G3K.

As the digger was driven through the security fence, it appears that the operators opened fire. The IED was detonated, destroying most of the police station and causing several casualties amongst those inside, but the van carrying the majority of the terrorists was raked with assault-rifle and GPMG fire. One terrorist attempted to escape across an adjoining field but was killed by an SAS cut-off group. Within moments, all eight terrorists were dead or dying.

The operation was not without its tragic consequences, however. A civilian car carrying two brothers dressed in boiler-suits, similar to those worn by the terrorists, was engaged by another SAS cut-off group who fired over 40 rounds into the car, killing one and severely wounding the other brother before the cut-off group realized their error. According to sources on both sides, at least one if not two PIRA cars were being used to reconnoitre

---

3 A friend of the author explained the differences between civilian law enforcement and military special operations thinking when he described a recent joint counter-terrorism exercise involving both police and Special Forces. He explained that whilst under police authority the terrorists were referred to as 'suspects'. Once authority was passed to the Army they were referred to as 'the enemy', with all the obvious connotations.

An extremely rare shot of the SAS in action in Afghanistan in 2014, carrying an ACOG-equipped L119A1 and an L7A2 GPMG; members of the Afghan SF can be seen in the right background. Operators had carried GPMGs for some rural ambushes in Northern Ireland when maximum firepower was required, such as against vehicles.

the planned route for the ASU, and the SAS had mistakenly believed the brothers' car to be one of those. A woman with a child was also caught in the crossfire, but was saved by a quick-thinking operator who dashed out of cover to haul her to safety.

Operation 'Flavius', Gibraltar

Operation 'Flavius' in March 1988 became perhaps the most controversial of SAS missions. A three-person PIRA Active Service Unit had been tracked to the British overseas territory of Gibraltar, where they were preparing to detonate a huge car bomb apparently targeting a military band from the Royal Anglian Regiment, in an attack that would kill and maim soldiers and tourists alike. MI5 had the targets under surveillance, and since the local police acknowledged that they lacked the tactical capacity to make safe arrests SAS assistance was requested. A small team from the on-call Special Projects element were dispatched to Gibraltar.

The operators carried concealed Browning pistols with four magazines per man, along with covert Push-To-Talk radios with earpieces. They were working under the (as it turned out, mistaken) belief that one or more of the terrorists was carrying a remote detonator to initiate the car bomb. There was also the reasonable suspicion that the ASU might well be armed. At a later inquest the soldiers claimed they had been briefed to arrest the terrorists and, once they were disarmed and restrained, to hand them over to an attached Royal Gibraltar Police officer. The rules of engagement for Operation 'Flavius' seemed to support this, but also spelled out circumstances when the SAS could fire without warning. As noted in Point 6, disclosed at the subsequent inquest: 'You and your men may fire without warning if the giving of a warning or any delay in firing could lead to death or injury to you … or any other person, or if giving of a warning is clearly impracticable'. A clear direction is noted in the Rules of Engagement (ROE) for a verbal warning to be issued before engaging: 'The warning is to be as clear as possible and is to include a direction to surrender and a clear warning that fire will be opened if the direction is not obeyed'.

Two SAS teams were deployed to attempt the arrests supported by a number of MI5 surveillance personnel. As one team closed in on their quarry, one of the terrorists apparently recognized them for what they were (the SAS had earlier been criticized by MI5 for looking too much like off-duty soldiers, in their near-identical 'bomber jackets' and jeans), and allegedly made a movement that one of the soldiers perceived as reaching for a weapon or for a detonator.

The soldier immediately opened fire with his pistol. Whatever the exact circumstances that precipitated the shooting, all three terrorists were engaged at close range, being repeatedly shot until they were on the ground with their hands visible. One terrorist was hit four times, another five, both including a characteristic SAS 'double tap' to the head; the third terrorist was shot at least 15 times by two operators, including a pair of double taps to the head as he was on the ground. In a grim testament to the effectiveness of SAS CQB training, not one round missed its intended target.

As a postscript, the presumed bomb car was most likely used only as a placeholder to reserve a parking space for the real bomb car, as no explosive device was found within it. However, several days after the shootings the Spanish police recovered another vehicle used by the ASU; this contained some 60kg of Czech Semtex plastic explosive, along with several hundred rounds of 7.62x39mm ammunition presumably for an AK47 assault rifle.

UNIFORMS & EQUIPMENT (III)

1: Sniper, B Squadron, 22 SAS; Afghanistan, 2010

Illustrated here is an SAS sniper in the cross-legged seated shooting stance, perhaps providing overwatch for an assault team hitting a Taliban compound, and armed with the Canadian PGW Timberwolf sniper rifle in .338 Lapua Magnum. The Timberwolf was selected by the Regiment during the late 2000s after a search for a lighter-weight and more modern rifle in this favoured calibre. This sniper wears an SAS smock in faded temperate-pattern DPM, and Crye G3 MultiCam combat trousers with built-in knee pads. Note the cutaway Oakley gloves, and issue Wiley X sunglasses pushed up onto the top of his head. His plate carrier is the Paraclete Special Operations Hard Plate Carrier (SOHPC).

2: Special Projects Team, 22 SAS; Hereford, 2008

This operator is shown in full CT intervention 'black kit'. His helmet is an RBR model, and he wears the fire-retardant black Nomex flight suit designed specifically for the unit, with integral knee pads (the original versions worn at the Iranian Embassy in 1980 were tank crew coveralls). The principal weapon is the suppressed Heckler & Koch MP5SD3 sub-machine gun equipped with weapon light, Aimpoint optic and forward grip. His secondary weapon is the SIG Sauer P226 pistol in a drop holster on his right thigh; note also the magazine pouch fixed to the left thigh. The drop holster was another SAS innovation, developed by the Operations Research Unit that worked with the CRW Wing to identify specific needs for the CT operator, which debuted at the Iranian Embassy. The original idea was to allow the operator easy access to the pistol while wearing the heavy assault armour that often included a groin protector, making accessing a traditional waistband holster difficult. The drop holster was also found to be ideal for use when abseiling down a building, as the operator could if necessary draw and fire his pistol while still 'on the rope'.

3: 22 SAS, Combined Joint Special Operations Task Force; Northern Iraq, 2014

As part of the covert UKSF presence in northern Iraq, both providing guidance for Coalition air strikes against Islamic State (ISIL) targets and mentoring Kurdish and Iraqi forces, this operator is shown wearing the now universal Crye MultiCam, with both an Under Body Armour Combat Shirt (UBACS) and Crye G3 combat trousers. The UBACS is a hybrid garment – a moisture-wicking T-shirt with long sleeves of standard combat shirt material – and in Crye versions it includes integrated elbow pads. Note that these items are in US MultiCam rather than the similar, MultiCam-derived British Multi Terrain Pattern (MTP). His plate carrier, also manufactured by Crye, is a MultiCam CAGE (Crye Assault Gear). He wears the Ops Core FAST Helmet with MultiCam cover, and attachment rails on either side that allow a range of lights, cameras and strobes to be mounted. The Ops Core helmet designs combine ballistic coverage with lighter weight and a more slimline profile, mating the convenience of the older non-ballistic 'skate' helmet with the heavier ballistic models. His primary weapon is the M6A2 Ultra Compact Individual Weapon (UCIW) with suppressor; Aimpoint Micro optic with swing-out Aimpoint magnifier behind it (allowing the operator to either use the sight in non-magnified CQB situations or as a magnified optic for longer-range shots); SureFire Scout weapon light, and a folding LWRC forward vertical grip.

Northern Ireland notwithstanding, in the decade after the Falklands War the Regiment appears to have seen little 'non-classified' action. Much of the 1980s was spent maintaining their reconnaissance and stay-behind role in West Germany in case Soviet forces ever crossed the border. (Author and SAS veteran Ken Connor spelt out the Regiment's intriguing role in any such Cold War Hot scenario: 'One squadron would be operating on the northern flank in Scandinavia and north-east Russia, one on the southern flank infiltrating from Turkey, one was to be held as a mobile reserve, and the fourth would be inserted into Russia and East Germany'.) At the same time they were developing and refining their CT capability, and dispatching training teams across the world to train friendly forces in small-unit COIN and CT techniques. One of the most contentious was the training of a number of Cambodian insurgent groups between 1985 and 1989 to fight against the Vietnamese People's Army, who were occupying Cambodia after ousting the murderous Khmer Rouge regime. Questions were raised as to the relationship between some of these groups and the Khmer Rouge. Although the SAS certainly did not directly train any Khmer Rouge, the country's murky factional politics (not dissimilar to those encountered in Afghanistan) cast a pall over the Regiment's involvement.

THE FIRST GULF WAR
Operation 'Granby', 1990–91

The Regiment almost missed out on Operation 'Granby', the United Kingdom's contribution to Operations 'Desert Shield' and 'Desert Storm'. Following the invasion of the oil-rich state of Kuwait by Saddam Hussein's Iraqi Army in August 1990, a coalition of Western and Arab nations led by the United States descended upon the region to protect Saudi Arabia from potential Iraqi aggression, and to liberate Kuwait.

The American Gen Norman Schwarzkopf, who headed up US Central Command, was far from an ardent supporter of special operations. His views had been coloured by his experiences in Vietnam, where he had seen Special

Members of the Regiment during build-up training in Saudi Arabia prior to crossing into Iraq for Operation 'Granby' in 1991. This atmospheric image shows an example of the Longline Light Strike Vehicle, a Unimog 'mothership' used to resupply patrols at desert rendezvous, the dirt bikes used for route reconnaissance, and, in the background, a Chinook helicopter of the RAF Special Forces Flight.

Operations Forces (SOF) missions go badly wrong, requiring conventional forces to ride to their rescue. He was adamant that SOF participation in Operation 'Desert Storm' would be limited, and conducted only with his personal agreement. A former commander of the Regiment, LtGen Sir Peter de la Billiere (known within the SAS as 'DLB') was Schwarzkopf's deputy, and was naturally keen to get his old unit into the fight. Although they had no formal mission, DLB nonetheless requested the deployment of the Regiment to the Middle East. Apart from G Sqn, who remained on SP duty in the United Kingdom, almost the entire 22 SAS deployed to the Gulf, including members from the Reserve R Sqn; to this day, it remains the largest SAS deployment since World War II. A squadron from the SBS, and the RAF's Special Forces Flight with four Chinook helicopters, deployed alongside the SAS component.[4]

Together, DLB and the commander of UKSF for Operation 'Granby' soon hatched a plan to convince Gen Schwarzkopf of the need for the SAS to develop options to release the large number of Western and Kuwaiti civilian workers then being held by Iraqi forces as human shields, but in December 1990 Saddam Hussein released the majority of the hostages and the prospective mission was scrubbed. Peter Ratcliffe, Regimental Sergeant Major of 22 SAS at the time, concluded that had the hostage rescue mission gone ahead it 'could only have ended in bloody nightmare, and many of us being shipped home in bodybags'. However, it had succeeded in putting the SAS on Schwarzkopf's radar.

General Schwarzkopf had agreed for US Army Special Forces and Marine Force Recon to conduct long-range reconnaissance missions to build up a picture of Iraqi troop movements and strengths. He was eventually convinced to allow the SAS to also deploy a handful of reconnaissance teams to monitor Main Supply Routes (MSRs), the key highways that crossed Iraq. It was Saddam Hussein's attempts to widen the war to include Israel, and thus shatter the delicate coalition of Arab nations arrayed against Iraq, that was directly responsible for a dramatic increase in operations for the Regiment.

'Scudbusting'

On 18 January 1991 the first eight of what would eventually total several dozen Iraqi SCUD-B ballistic missiles fell on Israel. With conventional high-explosive warheads, they inflicted only limited casualties; but they brought terror to Israeli streets, and threatened to bring Israel directly into the war – particularly if Saddam Hussein decided to arm future SCUDs with chemical warheads, as he had done during his war against Iran. Two dedicated flights of US Air Force F-15Es on 'SCUD Watch' could only be effective after the

---

4 One of the most unusual covert missions in Kuwait was only confirmed some 17 years later in the British Parliament. British Airways Flight 189 from London Heathrow to Kuala Lumpur via Kuwait City had been delayed for several hours in London on 1 August, 1990, allegedly due to technical issues; in fact, the delay may have been to allow a small SAS team to board the flight. According to affidavits from former UKSF soldiers read out in Parliament, the soldiers were part of an undercover mission codenamed 'Iscariot' tasked with 'gathering of intelligence material of Iraqi troop strengths, positions and unit identification'. Intriguingly, these affidavits identify the men not as members of the Regular or Territorial SAS but of 'the Increment', an alleged SIS (MI6) element that employed former UKSF members as contractors, in a similar fashion to the CIA Special Activities Division's Ground Branch. Whatever their exact origin, nine young men are recorded to have left the flight and subsequently disappeared after the remainder of the passengers and crew were interned by the Iraqis as they swept into Kuwait.

Images of UKSF activity during Operation 'Granby' are unavailable, so on these pages we show photos of the far better equipped and prepared operators who were deployed in southern Iraq for Operation 'Telic I' in 2003, and who fought the subsequent insurgency both in Baghdad and with Multi-National Division South-East around Basra. These soldiers display typical equipment for southern Iraq; one of them (right) wears a mix of British and American desert combats, and both have Paraclete RAV plate carriers in 'Ranger-green', with a mix of Paraclete and Blackhawk Industries pouches. The left-hand man has attached to the upper right of his vest 'chemlight' sticks and a clasp knife; below these are at least three grenade pouches for 'flashbangs'. Both L119A1 carbines feature sound suppressors and ACOG optics, and both SIG-Sauer pistols are carried in drop holsters rather than chest-mounted, as was more favoured by Task Force Black in Baghdad. In the background, members of an 'Armageddon' platoon from the resident infantry battalion are being briefed.

launch of the missiles (and questions have been raised over whether some of the targets they struck were in fact SCUD launchers at all).

According to historian Rick Atkinson, the SAS were deployed two days before the commencement of the air phase of Operation 'Desert Storm' on 17 January 1991, inserting three road-watch teams into western Iraq to establish observation of the MSR traffic. It was only when the SCUDs started to fall on Tel Aviv and Haifa on the 18th that the SAS were tasked with what became perhaps their most famous mission of the war – in DLB's words, 'You have one job... get those Scuds out of the battle'.

An operational area or 'SCUD Box', covering a huge swathe of western Iraq south of the main Highway 10 MSR, was allocated to the SAS and soon nicknamed 'SCUD Alley'; meanwhile their US counterparts from Delta

deployed to the north of Highway 10 in 'SCUD Boulevard'. Both SAS and Delta operations were initially hampered by delays in bringing strike aircraft onto the often time-sensitive targets – a problem that was only partially alleviated by the placing of Special Forces liaisons with the US Air Force in Riyadh. Dedicated flights were later instituted, kept stacked over the 'ops boxes' to further shorten the 'kill chain'.

Former SAS soldier and historian Michael Asher describes the assigned missions: 'The A and D Sqn mobile patrols received orders to track down Scuds and destroy them if possible, or vector-in strike aircraft. The half of B Sqn left at al-Jauf [in Saudi Arabia] were given a different task'. These three eight-man road-watch patrols would be inserted by helicopter to watch the three MSRs from covert observation posts.

The Bravo Two Zero controversy

The subsequently infamous 'Bravo Two Zero' was one such patrol. At least four accounts of this badly mishandled mission have been published, varying widely in some key details and timelines, so a single reconciled version is difficult to establish.

The decision was made to go in on foot as the terrain was regarded as being 'too flat for vehicles'. (Tellingly, the only patrol from the three road-watch missions that successfully infiltrated into Iraq was in fact equipped with short-wheelbase Land Rover 'Dinkies'). The other foot patrol landed, but requested and received an immediate Chinook extraction as soon as the patrol commander realized how flat and featureless the terrain actually was. Additionally, the Bravo Two Zero patrol apparently had to forage for 40mm grenades for their M203 launchers, and had to produce homemade Claymore mines as none were available. Mapping and provision of GPS units were both

An SAS strike team from Task Force Spartan in Basra, 2007. Note that they are using a lightly armoured Snatch 2 Land Rover, though it is fitted with an electronic countermeasures system to protect against improvised explosive devices. The operator in the centre wears what appears to be an American MICH helmet with a desert DPM cover, and a Paraclete plate carrier; his weapon is an ACOG-equipped L119A1. Note (right) the radio antenna tucked under the rear 'MOLLE' strips of the plate carrier.

A typically motley group of SAS operators from Operation 'Hathor'/Task Force Spartan preparing for an operation in southern Iraq in January 2007. Most clothing is British desert DPM, but one man (centre) wears American DCU-pattern trousers, another (second right) a black fleece, and one (far right) a temperate DPM smock. They carry L119A1s, some with sound suppressors, others with the CQB 'shorty' upper receiver and barrel.

woefully inadequate, and a lack of enough night-vision devices and any suppressed weapons were additional points of tension. The weather would also soon pose challenges: meteorological forecasts of extreme winter conditions with a strong chance of snow do not seem (almost incredibly) to have been communicated to the patrol. The members of the vehicle-mounted mobility patrols wore locally procured Bedouin coats against the cold weather. Michael Asher relates that 'polar winds thrashed unfettered across the Iraqi desert, and night temperatures plunged to freezing. The men hadn't come equipped for Arctic warfare – some of them hadn't even brought sleeping bags'.

Once the patrol was inserted, they discovered that they had been provided with the wrong radio frequencies and their radio messages were not getting through. They also found that they had been inserted close to an encamped Iraqi Army anti-aircraft battery. The next morning the patrol's hide was compromised by a civilian sheep-herder, who may or may not have informed the Iraqi Army. Convinced they were compromised, the patrol attempted to withdraw covertly, but were spotted by the enemy and broke contact under fire. Other accounts claim the patrol was actually approached by a small number of local farmers who fired several warning shots at them, thinking they were bandits. One participant's account spoke of Iraqi armoured vehicles and infantry, although this does not easily correlate with other contemporary accounts (including those of the Iraqi farmers, who were later interviewed).

As they withdrew the patrol commander used a TACBE line-of-sight emergency radio to broadcast their predicament to any passing Coalition aircraft, using the 'Turbo' callsign reserved for UK Special Forces. Unbeknown to the patrol, their initial messages had gotten through to SAS headquarters but – apparently due to a reluctance on the part of the leadership to confirm Gen Schwarzkopf's prejudiced view of special operations – no immediate extraction was authorized (although one version claims that a helicopter was dispatched, but that the mission had to be scrubbed when a pilot fell ill mid-flight).

After heading for a fixed emergency rendezvous (RV) with no sign of rescue, the patrol fell back on its previously decided Escape-and-Evasion plan, heading for the Syrian border (accounts also differ over whether this E&E plan was changed at some point, as when the SAS did finally start searching for the patrol they searched in the wrong area).

During the night march toward Syria, hampered by increasingly extreme weather, the ill-equipped patrol was separated into two halves. One half was forced to leave behind an operator, who died from hypothermia. The following morning the remaining two members of that element were compromised, and after a short firefight with Iraqi troops one of the operators ran out of ammunition and was captured. The second managed to escape and evade across the Syrian border, covering an astounding 186 miles on foot. The other half of the patrol was also eventually captured by the Iraqis, after losing another man in a firefight and a second to hypothermia after an attempt to swim across the Euphrates river. The captured men, and the one who had managed to escape into Syria, were eventually repatriated to the United Kingdom.

Vehicle-mounted patrols

Four mobile patrols or fighting columns were deployed, each consisting of one half of A and D Sqns equipped with six to eight of the famous 'Pinkie' Desert Patrol Vehicles (DPVs). They ranged far and wide across Iraq, and during one mission an operator reportedly destroyed a SCUD launcher with a vehicle-mounted Milan anti-tank guided missile. An Iraqi Army

An RAF loadmaster watches through his night-vision goggles for hostile fire as his Puma helicopter lifts off in Basra, 2008. During night insertions for house assaults the previous year Pumas had been involved in two fatal crashes involving the SAS. (Courtesy Cpl Ralph Merry RAF, UK MoD)

command-and-control site known as Victor Two was also attacked, with the SAS taking out bunkers with Milans and LAW (Light Anti-armour Weapon) rockets, and operators engaging in hand-to-hand combat with Iraqi soldiers. Complicating matters was the fact that the SAS had earlier crept into the facility and set a batch of demolition charges which were counting down toward detonation; the operators were forced to break cover and brave enemy fire to escape to their trucks before the charges blew.

Another mounted patrol encountered the proverbial fog of war. After bedding down for the night in a desert wadi, members of a D Sqn patrol were astounded to find themselves camped next to an Iraqi communications facility. They were quickly compromised by an Iraqi soldier wandering into their position, and all the SAS's weapons came into play during the subsequent fierce firefight against at least two regular Iraqi Army infantry platoons. The patrol managed to break contact in a fusillade of suppressive machine-gun and grenade-launcher fire, and after disabling two Iraqi 'technicals' (pick-up trucks) that had attempted to pursue them they made good their escape. The only problem was that during the chaos of the contact a supply Unimog had been immobilized by enemy fire and left behind. A patrol failed to find any trace of the seven-man crew, and the remaining vehicles drove to an emergency rendezvous. To their increasing alarm, the missing men didn't meet them there. They had in fact bailed out of the Unimog and captured one of the Iraqi technicals, using it to drive toward the border with Saudi Arabia. Eventually the bullet-pocked vehicle ground to a halt and the men were forced to march for five days, with a severely wounded comrade, before they reached the Saudi border.

Another operator was killed just days before the cessation of hostilities when he was shot in the chest during an ambush, bringing to four the number of SAS deaths during the conflict. Additionally five men were seriously wounded, and several captured. Considering the appalling state of mapping and reconnaissance imagery; poor intelligence on even fundamentals like the

D UNIFORMS & EQUIPMENT (IV)

1: Marksman, 1st Battalion, Parachute Regiment, Special Forces Support Group; Afghanistan, 2009

This SFSG operator is equipped for the marksman role within his platoon. He is carrying the 7.62x51mm Heckler & Koch HK417 with Schmidt & Bender scope, vertical forward grip, and SureFire sound suppressor. The HK417, the larger-calibre version of the venerable HK416, was procured specifically for UKSF; the rest of the British Army adopted the semi-automatic 7.62mm L129A1 some years later as their designated marksman rifle. His helmet is the SFSG-issue American MICH with an MSA Sordins radio headset; his uniform is in US-pattern Crye MultiCam, although his hooded SAS smock is of British design. He wears a Paraclete SOHPC plate carrier.

2: C Squadron, SBS; Iraq, 2004

This lightly equipped Special Boat Service operator is typical of the 2003–04 period, when the insurgency in Iraq had yet to fully ignite, and SAS and SBS operators could still move around Baghdad and Basra in Snatch Land Rovers or Defenders. The lack of a helmet and his general appearance are in stark contrast to Plate B3, which shows the level of arms and armour used by Task Force Black only 12 months later.

The operator carries a hand-camouflaged L119A1 with a weapon light mounted under the barrel and a magnified ACOG optic, and wears his P226 pistol in an Eagle drop holster. His uniform choice is unusual: the SAS smock is in faded temperate DPM, while his combat trousers in a desert-pattern 'tiger-stripe' are commercially acquired. He wears no visible body armour, although UKSF did have access to a number of covert vests. He wears a privately purchased Arktis chest rig, again in faded temperate DPM pattern, and has acquired an olive-drab Claymore mine bag to serve as a carryall and a 'dump pouch' for empty magazines.

3: Task Force 42, Z Squadron, SBS; Afghanistan, 2011

This SBS 'assaulter' on a kill-or-capture mission wears the Crye UBACS in MultiCam along with a pair of Crye G3 combat trousers. His plate carrier is the Paraclete SOHPC-SKD; note, attached to this, a Fairbairn-Sykes commando knife and a black CAT tourniquet. He sports both a subdued Union flag patch on the chest, and a second, infra-red reflective flag patch on his right sleeve. Open over the Paraclete plate carrier he wears an old DPM load-bearing PLCE assault vest with a CT3 radio handset at the left shoulder. His weapon is a fully accessorized L119A1 with suppressor, ACOG, Grip Pod forward grip/bipod, SureFire light, and PEQ-15 illuminator.

These two operators, pictured in April 2005, appear to be from M Sqn, SBS during the second and last Task Force Black rotation of the Special Boat Service. Note the black covert body armour worn under PLCE assault vests in temperate DPM. Both men wear American DCU combats, and both weapons mount thermal-imaging night-vision devices.

expected weather; and a distinct lack of essential kit such as night-vision goggles, TACBE radios and GPS units, it was only thanks to the individual skills and character of the SAS that more were not lost. Even the Deputy Director Special Forces was quoted as opining that on this occasion 'the Regiment forgot many of the lessons it had learned over the years'.

The Regiment had operated for some 43 days in the deserts of western Iraq. Their very presence appears to have been instrumental in stopping the SCUDs, since there were no further launches after only two days of SAS operations in their assigned 'box'. Despite this, significant questions remain over how many SCUDs were actually destroyed either from the air or on the ground. The Iraqis had deployed large numbers of East German-manufactured decoy vehicles, and apparently several oil tankers were erroneously targeted from the air. Despite a US Air Force study arguing that no actual SCUDs were destroyed, the SAS maintain that what they destroyed, often at relatively close range, certainly weren't decoys or oil tankers. The Regiment undoubtedly succeeded in forcing the SCUDs to move out of the 'SCUD Box' and into the north-west of Iraq; and the increased distances, for an already inaccurate and unreliable missile system, effectively eliminated the SCUD threat. General Schwarzkopf sent a personal message thanking Delta and the Regiment: 'You guys kept Israel out of the war'.

During Operation 'Granby' the SAS also perfected desert mobility techniques that would influence US Army Special Forces during initial operations in Afghanistan and Iraq a decade later. SAS Mobility operators used the 'mothership' concept to resupply their mounted patrols. Along with the DPVs, a number of cut-down Unimog and ACMAT VLRA trucks were infiltrated into the area of operations and served as mobile resupply points, themselves being stocked with fuel, ammunition and water by RAF Chinook drops. This meant that the SAS mobility patrols could effectively stay in the field indefinitely.

* * *

One of the other effects of the SAS contribution to Operation 'Granby' and the subsequent publication of a number of memoirs (by members of the doomed Bravo Two Zero patrol, among others) was the introduction of confidentiality agreements. These meant that serving members could no longer publish memoirs or accounts without the prior agreement of the Ministry of Defence. Soldiers who refused to sign these agreements faced being 'RTU'd' (returned to unit), the gravest fear of any serving SAS operator. One surviving member of Bravo Two Zero, who was wounded twice during the operation, was even pursued through the New Zealand courts to have his book stopped. Those who did publish their experiences, or were suspected of having been sources for journalists, were blacklisted and cut off from any association with Hereford.

THE BALKANS, 1994–*c*.1999

In 1994–95 LtGen Mike Rose, who had been both CO of 22 SAS and Director Special Forces (DSF) during the 1980s, commanded the United Nations Protection Force (UNPROFOR) mission in Bosnia-Herzegovina, part of the violently fragmented former Yugoslavia. Needing a realistic appreciation of the situation in a number of UN-mandated 'safe areas' that were surrounded by Bosnian-Serb forces, he requested and received elements from both A and D Squadrons. These deployed with standard British Army uniforms, UN blue berets and L85A1 (SA80) assault rifles, to 'hide in plain sight' under official cover as UK Liaison Officers for the general. They established the 'ground truth' in the besieged enclaves, and, being trained as Forward Air Controllers, they took with them laser target designators to guide in NATO aircraft should the decision be made to engage the Bosnian-Serb ground forces.

In Goražde an SAS operator, in UN dress, was shot and killed as a patrol attempted to survey Bosnian-Serb positions. Later, a Royal Navy Sea Harrier FRS.1 of 801 NAS from HMS *Ark Royal* was shot down on 16 April 1994 with a Serbian SA-7 SAM, but its pilot, Lt Nick Richardson, was rescued by a four-man SAS team operating within the besieged city. The same team called in a number of air strikes on armoured columns entering the city, until they were forced to escape through the lines of encircling Serbian

Two members of D Squadron in Sierra Leone in 2000 for Operation 'Barras'. The left-hand trooper carries a Minimi Para LMG , his mate a Diemaco C7A2.

paramilitaries to avoid capture and possible execution.

A small SAS reconnaissance team of only a pair of operators was also covertly inserted, wearing UN blue berets, into the UN 'safe area' of Srebrenica where a Dutch UN battalion was supposedly protecting the population and thousands of Muslim refugees from threatening Bosnian-Serb forces. The SAS team attempted to call in air strikes as Serbian forces attacked, but were frustrated by UN bureaucracy and ineptitude. They were finally ordered to withdraw, and the city fell to the Bosnian-Serb Army (VRS) led by Gen Ratko Mladić, resulting in the genocidal execution of some 8,000 civilians. The full story of the SAS's doomed involvement in Srebrenica may never be known; the SAS patrol commander wrote a series of newspaper articles about the tragedy, but was successfully taken to court by the MoD in 2002 to stop publication.

In the aftermath of the Dayton Agreement of December 1995 the SAS remained active in the region, alongside US Joint Special Operations Command (JSOC) units, in the hunt for war criminals on behalf of the International Criminal Tribunal for the Former Yugoslavia. One such operation in July 1997 resulted in the capture of one fugitive and the death of another when he opened fire on a plain-clothes SAS team. Another wanted war criminal was captured by the Regiment in November 1998 from a remote safe house in Serbia; he was driven to the Drina river separating Serbia from Bosnia before being transported across in an SAS Zodiac inflatable boat and helicoptered out of the country.

The SAS also deployed D Sqn to Kosovo in 1999 to guide in air strikes by NATO aircraft and reconnoitre potential avenues of approach should a NATO ground force be committed. Apparently an RAF Hercules carrying several 'Pinkies' and an SAS contingent on their way to reconnoitre Slatina Airport, outside the capital Pristina, crashed on take-off from Kukës air base in Albania on 11 June 1999, injuring several men. Members of G Sqn were later dispatched into Kosovo from Macedonia to conduct advanced-force operations and assist in securing a number of bridgeheads in preparation for the larger NATO incursion. Informed rumours also persist that the Regiment were heavily involved in training and mentoring the Kosovo Liberation

Army, a paramilitary force of ethnic Albanians fighting for independence for Kosovo.

OPERATION 'BARRAS', 2000

This operation in September 2000 would mark the first time that the SAS were deployed to rescue members of the British Army. In the war-torn West African nation of Sierra Leone, 'Barras' was the codename for the rescue of five members of 1st Bn Royal Irish Regt and a local liaison officer, who had been ambushed and taken hostage by a local militia group known in media accounts as the West Side 'Boys' (a sanitized version of their actual 'gangsta' name). This was one of the main insurgent groups within the so-called Revolutionary United Front (RUF), a loose and atrociously violent movement then waging civil war against the elected government of Sierra Leone. They had ambushed the British patrol with both superior firepower, including a 'technical' mounting a 14.5mm ZPU-2 cannon, and child soldiers whom the Royal Irish soldiers were naturally unwilling to engage. (Indeed, many of the RUF's fighters were abducted children, forced to fight for the group and controlled with alcohol and drugs.) In the ambush of the Royal Irish a total of 11 hostages had initially been taken, but six were released during protracted negotiations.

The SAS and elements of the SBS had already deployed to Sierra Leone in support of wider British military efforts against the insurgent RUF (Operation 'Palliser'), and had been on stand-by to effect the relief of a British Army major and his team of UN observers from a besieged jungle camp. Additionally they had conducted their traditional role of covert reconnaissance, sizing up the strengths and dispositions of the rebel forces. D Squadron had been dispatched in case a hostage-rescue operation should be mounted. Supporting them would be elements from 1st Bn Parachute Regt (1 Para), who had a symbiotic relationship with UKSF that would eventually be cemented by the formation of the Special Forces Support Group (SFSG) in 2005. As negotiations stalled and the hostages were subjected to mock executions, Prime Minister Tony Blair authorized a rescue mission.

The West Side Boys' headquarters was in the village of Gberi Bana in an area known as Rokel Creek. Across the creek was the second, larger village of Magbeni where many of the fighters and camp-followers lived. The planners worried about the three captured British WMIK Land Rovers, one of which mounted a .50cal Browning heavy machine gun that could easily shoot down a hovering Chinook. Additionally, the West Side Boys had several 12.7mm DShK heavy machine guns deployed around the camp. The SAS had established a number of covert OPs around the periphery of Gberi Bana, and conducted pattern-of-life surveillance to build up an accurate picture of the location, demeanour and armament of the West Side Boys. They also confirmed the location of the hostages; but it became apparent that the rebels were intending to move them to another location deeper in the jungle, and may have been negotiating to sell them to the main RUF, which had a gruesome reputation. At a report of this development, a military rescue operation was approved by the Prime Minister. Colonel Tim Collins of 1st Royal Irish explained the operational plan as follows in his autobiography:

> The Chinooks would suppress known enemy billets on their approach, and their door gunners would take down the 12.7mm heavy machine guns as they landed on the football pitch. SAS teams

A UKSF operator from an unidentified unit in Afghanistan, 2005. He fires an ACOG-equipped L119A1 with CQB barrel, and appears to wear a Paraclete plate carrier.

already in place would provide covering fire. Simultaneously, Lynx helicopters from the Special Forces detachment would strafe the area to the south of the river, preventing use of the captured vehicles and more importantly the captured machine gun, keeping reinforcements at bay and creating an opportunity for the Para distraction force to land and assault the rebel village...

The main assault troops, guided from the football pitch by the observation teams already in place, would close in on the hostages and take them to safety. A four-man team would go after Kallay [the rebel leader]. We wanted him alive. A sixteen-strong troop would cover the rescue force and dispatch any West Side Boys who tried to interfere.

At dawn on Sunday, 10 September 2000 the assault was launched. The SAS observation team engaged a number of rebels who attempted to enter the house where the hostages were being held, while the hostage-rescue team fast-roped to the ground. Despite this, a number of rocket-propelled grenades (RPGs) were launched at the hovering Chinooks. Moments later the SAS had killed the captors and secured the hostages, who were then raced toward the disused football pitch designated as the extraction point. During the fierce firefight one SAS soldier was hit by an enemy round that skirted his body armour; he too was evacuated to the LZ, with an SAS medic working feverishly to save his life.

Meanwhile, A Coy of 1 Para landed in swampland to the west of Magbeni, across the water from the SAS. They advanced in a textbook cordon-and-clearance of the village, engaging all who put up a fight. Above, Lynx gunships kept up a heavy fire at the West Side Boys' heavy weapons, while a Sierra Leone Air Force Mi-24 Hind-D gunship, flown by a South African mercenary crew, raked the jungle with cannon and rocket fire. Despite determined resistance, the Paras managed to secure the village at a cost of about a dozen wounded. Officially, the West Side Boys suffered 25 fatalities; unofficially, the number is thought to be closer to 80.

All the hostages were safely rescued, a result marred only by the death of the wounded SAS trooper after he was evacuated to a Royal Navy ship. The MoD's press release included a statement from the Prime Minister paying tribute to 'the skill, the professionalism and the courage of the armed forces involved'. Predictably, no mention was made of SAS involvement, with the operation attributed solely to 'elements of the 1st Battalion of the Parachute Regiment, Lynx attack helicopters and RAF Chinook helicopters'.

AFGHANISTAN, 2001–2006

In the wake of the attacks on the United States on 11 September, 2001 the United Kingdom was amongst the first nations to pledge unilateral military support, and a key component of that support was UK Special Forces. According to popular rumour the Regiment (or at least, former members contracted by the SIS) had already been in Afghanistan during the Soviet-Afghan War of the 1980s, training members of the anti-Soviet *mujahideen*.

In mid-October 2001, members of both A and G Sqns of 22 SAS, with reinforcements from 21 and 23 SAS, deployed to Afghanistan in support of

A member of 22 SAS is trained by a US combat controller in the use of the Special Operations Forces Laser Aiming Module (SOFLAM) target designator. Assisting air target acquisition is now a core task for Special Operations Forces. (Courtesy SRA Rick Bloom, USAF)

the US military's Operation 'Enduring Freedom' (at that time D Sqn was on SP duty, while B Sqn was overseas on a long-term training exercise). The operations that they were initially allotted were disappointing, being relatively straightforward reconnaissance tasks. Despite dramatic media reports to the contrary, no SAS soldiers were involved in the December fighting at Tora Bora, hunting Osama bin Laden. A small contingent of SBS operators did work alongside a Delta Force squadron, but the tales of close-quarter gunfights in al Qaeda cave complexes were simply products of journalists' fevered imaginations. Far from being in the thick of the action, it was only through the personal intervention of the DSF and the Prime Minister himself that the SAS saw any significant action at all.

Operation 'Trent' became the largest single SAS operation, with the majority of both squadrons conducting a daring (some might say foolhardy) daylight ground assault, without prior close reconnaissance, on a heavily guarded opium-processing facility south-west of Kandahar. A patrol of G Sqn's Air Troop HALO-parachuted into remote desert flats to establish an airhead for the rest of the assault force. Landing in C-130 Hercules transports, A and G Sqns, mounted in 38 'Pinkie' DPVs and two logistics vehicles, drove to a forming-up point and prepared to conduct the assault. G Squadron would provide the Fire Support Base armed with machine guns, mortars and Milan anti-tank guided missiles, 'shooting in' the mounted assault by A Sqn; once on the objective A Sqn would dismount, and conduct standard infantry clearance of the site. Incredibly, only one hour of on-call close air support had been allotted. The operation was opened by an air strike, followed by a bombardment of 81mm mortar bombs from G Sqn as A Sqn raced toward their objective. They soon overcame concerted resistance, and the facility was captured. Several men were wounded including the RSM, while others were saved by their body armour and helmets. The commander of G Sqn, who later received the Military Cross, was struck by four bullets, none of which penetrated his body armour. Disaster was narrowly avoided when a US air strike almost hit the G Sqn positions.

SAS veteran Ken Connor has commented that: 'The SAS are strategic troops; if there is no specific task for them, they should not be used'. By all accounts, Operation 'Trent' was hardly a strategic mission, and perhaps should have been conducted by conventional infantry or a unit such as the US Army Rangers. It seems to have been largely a matter of the SAS being offered a 'take-it-or-leave-it' chance to get into the fight in Afghanistan, regardless of the importance of the target or the inadequacy of the preparations.

Thereafter 22 SAS did maintain a troop-strength presence in Afghanistan, drawn from whichever squadron was deployed to Iraq, but this arrangement officially ended in 2006, when the DSF allocated Iraq to the SAS and Afghanistan to the Special Boat Service. (The American LtGen Stanley McChrystal, head of Joint Special Operations Command, had set a similar demarcation in 2005, with Delta assigned to Iraq, and SEAL Team Six and the Rangers allocated rotating command in Afghanistan.) Territorial soldiers of 21 and 23 SAS continued to operate in Afghanistan, providing both close protection for SIS officers and training the fledgling Afghan National Army (ANA) and Afghan National Police (ANP). They were also instrumental in early efforts to unite various warlord factions in concert with the Secret Intelligence Service. In June 2008, three members of 23 SAS were killed alongside a female Army Intelligence corporal near Lashkar Gah when an IED destroyed their lightly armoured Snatch Land Rover. The Territorials continued in their training role, largely focusing on the ANP, until 2010, when the task was handed over to regular British Army units.

IRAQ, 2003–2009
Operation 'Row'

This was the codename for the UKSF contribution to Operation 'Telic', the British invasion of Iraq in 2003, which ultimately led to a six-year COIN war against determined enemies. UK Special Forces were organized into two distinct task forces: Task Force 14 was based around two squadrons from the SAS, and the SBS provided Task Force 7. Their initial missions were to ascertain Iraqi troop dispositions and strengths, to strike strategic targets, and – in the case of one SBS mission – to attempt to negotiate the surrender of Iraqi units. The SAS were also tasked with carrying out harassing raids to keep the enemy guessing as to the true intentions of Coalition Forces.

The majority of B and D Sqns crossed the border from Jordan on the night of 17 March 2003, as part of a ground assault on a suspected chemical munitions site at a water-treatment plant in the city of al Qa'im in the western Iraqi desert (it has also been reported that this might have been a SCUD launch site or depot). An SAS officer was quoted by author Mark Nicol as

 VEHICLES (1)

1: 'Pinkie' – Land Rover 110 Desert Patrol Vehicle (DPV)
The DPV was the successor to the famous Series IIA 'Pink Panther' used by the Regiment since the 1960s. The original vehicles were painted in a salmon-pink shade that was judged to be the best camouflage colour for the open desert; while the DPVs were painted in standard British sand, they were still reverently referred to as 'Pinkies'. Our example shows a typical DPV toward the end of its service life in c.2003, armed with the standard .50cal M2 Browning heavy machine gun and forward-mounted 7.62x51mm L7A2 GPMG.

2: Longline Light Strike Vehicle (LSV)
The illustrated vehicle is the Mk 2 four-wheel drive version of the LSV, painted in standard British sand with dark grey camouflage stripes. The LSV has entered the popular imagination as a prototypical SAS vehicle, but there is still significant controversy over whether any LSVs actually crossed into Iraq in 2003. Certainly the vehicles were forward-deployed and featured in squadron build-up training, but due to their reported poor payload capacity and relatively fragile chassis they were apparently hastily replaced with short-wheelbase Land Rover 90 'Dinkies'.

1

2

This photo is believed to show SBS operators during the early stages of Operation 'Row' in southern Iraq, 2003; they wear a mix of DPM and American DCU combats, and PLCE assault vests. The vehicles ahead of the 'mothership' appear to be modified WMIKs rather than 'Pinkies'. Both the SBS and SAS would replace their Land Rover platforms in 2004 with the Project Menacity SRV/OAVs.

saying: 'D Squadron would be flying in 6x CH-47s in 3x waves, 120 kilometres over the border... It was a location where missiles had been fired at Israel in the past, and a site of strategic importance for WMD material. D Squadron comprised 60 men.' The three pairs of Chinooks carried the majority of D Sqn along with their 'Pinkie' DPVs (the Iraq invasion would be the vehicles' last mission before retirement). The squadron established a patrol laager at a remote desert location outside al Qa'im, and awaited the arrival of B Sqn who had driven overland from Jordan. Their approach to the plant was compromised, and a firefight developed which ended in one 'Pinkie' having to be abandoned and destroyed. Repeated attempts to assault the plant were driven back, leading to the SAS calling in an air strike which finally silenced the opposition.

Meanwhile, 16 Troop of D Sqn had conducted a mounted reconnaissance of an Iraqi Army facility near the Syrian border, followed by a harassing attack on the site. Two other troops had conducted mobile ambushes on Iraqi units in the area, although they themselves were being hunted by a large Fedayeen Saddam unit mounted in 'technicals'. Both squadrons were also later involved in conducting interdictions of fleeing Iraqi leadership targets on the MSR heading for Syria.

Task Force 14 operated in close cooperation with the Delta Force-based Task Force 20, and Task Force 64 based on the Australian SAS Regiment (SASR). Compared to their initial experiences in Afghanistan, the SAS were far more integrated into the Iraq operation and were deployed on largely strategic tasks. On 21 March two Iraqi airfields, codenamed H2 and H3, were captured by the SAS working alongside 1 Sqn SASR. In the south, several small teams from D Sqn also conducted forward route reconnaissance in support of the main British offensive. UK Special Forces suffered no losses during these operations.

Newspaper reports at the time claimed that an SAS element had been compromised in northern Iraq, leaving behind a 'Pinkie', a quad bike and a Stinger SAM missile to be captured and paraded on Iraqi television. This was in fact M Sqn of the SBS, who were ambushed by a far larger Fedayeen Saddam hunter force supported by Iraqi armour. The operators were forced to scatter to break out and fought running battles until they could be extracted (or, in one memorable case, drove to the Syrian border on a quad bike, shadowed by US Air Force F-16s to slow down their pursuers). The captured DPV was the result of a failed detonator on a bar mine set to destroy the vehicle, and the SBS were unfairly criticised for their conduct during this operation.

Once hostilities ceased the SAS relocated to the capital, Baghdad, and began to look for work. B and D Squadrons conducted support operations for the SIS before being rotated home, to be replaced by G Squadron. Due to their responsibility for both Iraq and Afghanistan, this squadron only numbered between 20 and 30 operators on the ground in Iraq with another dozen or so in Afghanistan, according to the author Mark Urban. But the inadequately thought-through war in Iraq was only just beginning, and in just six months a nexus of Iraqi nationalist insurgents, foreign jihadists and former Ba'ath Party members would begin to tear the country apart.

Task Force Black/Task Force Knight:

Ops 'Paradoxical' & 'Crichton'

In a move that would help cement their relationship with Delta, the SAS squadron took up residence in one of Saddam Hussein's former palaces on the Tigris river, right next door to Delta and close to the Rangers of Task Force Red; they even smashed a hole through an adjoining wall to allow easy access between the Delta and SAS camps. At the back of the properties a secured helipad was built, allowing American MH-60 Black Hawks and MH-6 Little Birds of the 160th Special Operations Aviation Regt (the famous 'Night Stalkers'), and later Lynxes and Pumas of the British Joint Special Forces Aviation Wing, access to pick up assault and sniper teams setting out

SAS assaulters from Task Force Black in Iraq, 2006, wearing American ACU and DCU-pattern uniforms, and Ranger-green Paraclete RAV plate carriers with chest-mounted holsters for their SIG-Sauer P226 pistols. Night-vision devices mounted on their MICH helmets are worn here flipped up out of the way. The carbine of the right-hand soldier has the EOTech 551 optic favoured by the Regiment's colleagues of Delta Force, rather than the more usual British-issue ACOG.

Task Force Knight operators photographed early in 2007, when they were heavily committed against the al Qaeda car-bomb network in Baghdad; an esoteric mix of mainly US camouflage patterns is evident. To judge from his just-visible backpack, the soldier on the right wearing a temperate DPM smock appears to be a medic. Note the sound suppressors on the carbines; the Regiment made increasing use of these in Iraq, principally to reduce the amplified noise from firing inside buildings rather than for any covert application. Several patches have been blacked out here for security reasons, as has a tactical aide-memoire fixed to the left forearm (second left). The left-hand operator's L119A1 shows hand-painted camouflage in sand and green.

on nightly raids. The SAS continued to operate as Task Force 14 until 2004, when they were renamed Task Force Black (Delta were known as Task Force Green, and the SEALs as Task Force Blue). The SAS presence was built around a core squadron eventually supported by a company from the SFSG (known as Task Force Maroon), and the secretive Joint Support Group; this conducted human intelligence-gathering, and included a team of specially trained Iraqis known as 'the Apostles'. Under Operation 'Paradoxical' the SAS were granted a new remit to operate on COIN and CT missions within Iraq; the mission would be renamed as Operation 'Crichton' in 2005.

Task Force Black was given a target list of Former Regime Elements (FRE) to track down, including members of the infamous 'card deck' of high-value targets which they began to target as early as June 2003 (though these initial targets were felt to be hardly the pick of the litter). The Regiment was also involved in the hunt for the killers of six Royal Military Police at Majar al-Kabir in southern Iraq in June 2003. Despite being warned of the potential for reigniting the violence that had ended in the RMPs' deaths, an SAS element flew down from Baghdad to conduct Operation 'Jocal', their own investigation into who was responsible for the murders. SAS operators wore the distinctive RMP red beret and MP brassard, to mimic members of the fallen soldiers' unit and perhaps garner sympathy with the local Iraqi police and civilian population. Their ruse would not have fooled anyone with a passing familiarity with UKSF, since these 'Redcaps' carried Diemaco carbines instead of issue SA80s.

The Regiment's first operation outside the FRE target list was Operation 'Abalone' by A Sqn in October 2003. Targeting a foreign-fighter 'facilitator' in Ramadi, the operation would become memorable for all the wrong

reasons. During the initial assault on one target house a number of SAS soldiers were hit by small-arms and RPG fire from within, and an attached SBS operator was killed. Eventually Delta stepped in to assist, and the target houses were secured.

The SAS deployment was expanding as RAF Chinook support was provided, allowing them a certain degree of independence from the Americans. During a house assault in Baghdad in February 2004 they narrowly missed their primary target, the Jordanian terrorist Abu Musab al-Zarqawi, then leader of al Qaeda in Iraq and future inspiration for the so-called 'Islamic State in Iraq and the Levant' (ISIL). They did, however, capture or kill a wide range of foreign fighters, from Sudanese to Pakistanis (and on one occasion they mistakenly 'lifted' an Iraqi CIA asset).

As the operational tempo increased, the Regiment refined their tactics. These ranged from vehicle interdictions where targets were engaged by snipers perched in helicopters overhead, to more common instances of what the British termed 'house assaults'. These were bread-and-butter operations for the SAS, who became skilled in a range of techniques to gain access to targets. Their methods of entry ranged from 'soft knocks', where the assaulters made a silent approach and entry, to more dynamic entries using explosive frame charges, or vehicles to ram through walls. As the number of dedicated helicopters increased, these tactics extended to dropping teams onto the roof of a target house. Following successful trials by Delta, the SAS also began to incorporate a relatively new form of force-multiplier into their ranks: the Combat Assault Dog (CAD), which would often be sent into a target house with the assaulters.

The roadside-bomb threat increased as the insurgency gained pace, with SAS teams being attacked on the way to and from their targets. Their 'Pinkies' and Snatch Land Rovers were replaced in 2005 by borrowed Humvees that afforded some protection against bomb and bullet. Delta used a six-wheeled armoured truck called a Pandur, and the SAS requested the same vehicle. The manufacturer apparently could not turn around the request fast enough, so instead they purchased the Australian Bushmaster Protected Mobility Vehicle (PMV) in a modified version known as the Escapade.

Operation 'Traction'
The SAS commander continued to push for greater integration into the JSOC operation until eventually the Regiment were allowed to target the same mission set as Delta, namely Sunni insurgents and al Qaeda in Iraq. In

LEFT
Two SAS operators at Mission Support Site Fernandez, the joint US/British SOF helipad in Baghdad, in 2007. Just visible under magnification, on the right hand soldier's plate carrier, is a 'F**k al Qaeda'/Stars-and-Stripes patch, as worn by Delta – a Union flag version was quickly acquired. Such patches became so common that even the Regiment's then-CO was seen sporting a subdued-colour version, plus G Sqn's 'Punisher' skull-and-G patch. Other squadron patches included A Sqn's red scorpion design. The infra-red chemical light-sticks carried by the left-hand man were used both to mark landing zones, and to indicate rooms within a target house that had been cleared and secured.

RIGHT
A blurred but interesting shot of an SAS assault element perched on the pod seats of an American MH-6 Little Bird of 160th Special Operations Aviation Regt, lifting off from the joint helipad at Mission Support Site Fernandez.

One of only two known images of the armoured 4x4 Bushmaster Escapade vehicle in SAS service, here in the dust of Iraq in 2008. It is equipped with a Kongsberg Protector remote weapons station, but also has prominent wire-cutter bars to protect the commander when he is exposed. The vehicle is fitted with custom bull bars designed to allow it to breach the wall of a target building, added appliqué armour, and a suite of counter-IED electronics. In all, 24 Bushmasters were procured for the Regiment.

January 2006, under Operation 'Traction', Task Force Black became for all practical purposes an additional Delta squadron, as they deployed an SAS Task Group HQ at Balad alongside the JSOC headquarters. They also gained increased helicopter surveillance capabilities including a number of attached Pumas and Lynxes, but did not yet have their own Unmanned Aerial Vehicles (UAVs), so had to rely on manned reconnaissance aircraft.

(Previously, the integration with Delta had been stalled by two problems: differences in the ROE between the British and American units – the British ROE appeared to be far more restrictive – and the treatment of detainees captured by the SAS but handed over to Joint Special Operations Command. Several American operators had been disciplined, and some sacked from their units, after roughing up detainees captured by the strike teams (including the use of Tasers). Additionally, some foreign jihadists captured by the SAS had been 'rendered' into the CIA network of 'black sites' and subsequently tortured, and the British were not comfortable with UKSF being involved in these 'extraordinary renditions'.)

Lieutenant-General McChrystal's plan was summed up by the acronym F3EA or 'Find-Fix-Finish-Exploit-Analyse'. In simple terms, this meant identifying a valid terrorist target (Find); confirming his physical location (Fix); raiding that location to capture or kill the individual (Finish);

F **VEHICLES (II)**

1: Menacity Surveillance & Reconnaissance Vehicle/ Offensive Action Vehicle (SRV/OAV)

The version illustrated here shows a typical twin GPMG mount that has proven popular with the SAS as a vehicle-mounted weapon ever since Operation 'Granby' in 1990–91. The Menacity also features a swing-out MG mount for the front passenger, and note that this example has a Javelin anti-tank missile among the lavish amounts of stowage carried for long operations. Air-portable by Chinook or Hercules, the original Special Forces version was essentially soft-skinned, although appliqué armour was later added. Additions after experience in Afghanistan included extra belly armour to counter IEDs, and seats designed to channel any explosive blast away from the crew.

2: Toyota Hilux Non Standard Tactical Vehicle (NSTV)

In common with American SOF units, the SAS have also deployed in both Afghanistan and Iraq in civilian pick-up trucks. This camouflage-painted example from Afghanistan, c.2008, is fitted with a satellite communications array and an anti-IED electronic countermeasures system mounted on a false roof; an L7A2 GPMG fixed to the roll bar; aftermarket bull bars with attached sand channel to assist if the vehicle becomes bogged down; and extra-wide sand tyres. The SAS normally use the Toyota Hilux, although Ford Rangers acquired from the Afghan National Police, and locally purchased Mitsubishis, have also been seen. In 2014 the Regiment purchased 60 such vehicles to supplement those in-theatre.

1

2

Another poor-quality but interesting shot, showing 22 SAS/Task Force Black assaulters inside an objective. They wear a mix of American ACU pattern, MultiCam and desert DPM. Just visible (second left, and centre, high on the plate carriers) is G Sqn's 'Punisher' patch, showing 'G' on the cranium of an elongated yellow skull on a black disc. The right-hand man sports a full-colour 'F**k al Qaeda'/Union flag patch on the left side of his plate carrier.

conducting a search for intelligence at the location (Exploit); and examining and interpreting that intelligence (Analyse). He instructed his strike teams to conduct Sensitive Site Exploitations (SSEs) at their target sites – literally bagging up hard drives, laptops, paperwork and, most importantly, mobile phones. As the operation matured and LtGen McChrystal managed to develop a multi-agency network to support his assaulters, including support from the US intelligence community and FBI, so their SSE methods matured. Instead of piling everything into a garbage bag, items (including dead and captured terrorists) were photographed in-place before being processed using procedures similar to those of a crime lab, so that the investigators and analysts could ascertain any hidden connections.

Indeed, the JSOC operation was eventually supported by real-time interception capabilities against any mobile phone operating in Iraq. The assault teams were equipped with a handheld 'magic wand' that allowed direction-finding based on specific mobile-phone transmissions. It has been reported that the American National Security Agency could locate any mobile phone linked to a JSOC or SAS target; JSOC could then analyse where the phone had been, who it had 'talked' to, and for how long. Combined with physical intelligence recovered from target sites and by long-loiter UAV surveillance, patterns of movement and associations with other terrorists and insurgents could be established and then exploited.[5]

Often the SAS operators were conducting three or four raids every night, becoming a nocturnal strike force that slept and refitted during the day, waking in the afternoon for briefings on the target folders that the intelligence and targeting cells had developed, which were often based on recovered intelligence from the previous night's jobs. Lieutenant-General McChrystal and the SAS commander sometimes joined assault teams from the US Special Operations Forces and the SAS on night raids. The Regiment, and the SFSG, often wore American Army Combat Uniform (ACU) or the earlier Desert Camouflage Uniform (DCU) the better to blend in when operating alongside American JSOC units. Like their counterparts in Delta, the SAS also preferred

5 According to the former CO of 22 SAS, if the target could not by any means be captured, e.g. if a team could not be flown to his location in time to effect a capture, or if such an operation was deemed too risky for the operators involved, then those 'designated as terrorists' would be engaged by stand-off means, i.e. an air strike, either from an armed UAV or a conventional aircraft.

a non-conventional look, often mixing-and-matching various American and British-issue and commercial items (which would, in fact, make them stand out as Special Forces).

The brutal pace of the raids and the increased focus on the al Qaeda target list inevitably resulted in casualties. One SAS sergeant miraculously survived being shot in the face at point-blank range with an AK47 assault rifle, while another was blown off a roof by an exploding suicide bomber. Tours of deployment were originally for four months, but this was increased to six months; the Regiment felt that operators thus developed a better understanding of the operational environment, but it also led to an increased psychological toll. Delta were also suffering significant casualties, with six dead in one three-month period; in fact, Gen McChrystal asked for SAS operators to help 'bring up the numbers' in his depleted squadrons.

Basra: Operations 'Hathor' & 'Spartan'

The Regiment also supported the British Task Force in southern Iraq, with a small detachment based in Basra. Known as Operation 'Hathor', their main tasks were to provide direct support to the SIS in the south, and to conduct close target reconnaissance for Task Force Black strike operations. For a number of years the Basra presence was literally a handful of operators, and was viewed by many as a distant second choice to the high-tempo ops of Task Force Black. Operation 'Hathor' was eventually increased in size by 2007; renamed Task Force Spartan, it conducted strike operations against both Shia insurgents and their Iranian sponsors.

Toyota Hilux pick-up truck as modified for use in Afghanistan; compare with Plate F2.

An excellent detail shot of a Task Force Knight operator in Baghdad wearing a DPM-pattern hooded SAS smock; some patches have been blacked out for security reasons. The MICH helmet has AN/PVS-21 night-vision equipment; the bright patch on the side is an IR-visible 'glint patch' for friend/foe identification. The armour vest is the Paraclete RAV in 'Ranger green'. The CT3 handset at his left shoulder is connected to his Peltor headset, and to a Racal Cougar radio set in a rear pouch. Just visible above his right shoulder is an early blast meter, which records the concussive impact of an IED as an aid to any medical treatment. Attached at top front centre of the RAV is a Petzl headlamp, and the bundles of white cubes each side of it are the ends of plastic cable-ties for restraining detainees. Both the Regiment and Delta adopted chest rigs for their pistols: these did not snag on obstructions like door or window frames, and allowed just as fast a draw when transitioning from primary to secondary weapon. Magazine pouches are attached at the sides of the RAV and 'flashbang' grenade pouches at the front; a pistol magazine is tucked in on the right. The vertical black item down his right chest is a field-expedient single-point sling for his carbine, which will hold the weapon in place at waist level.

Operation 'Spartan' was supported by Armageddon Platoon, a cordon and quick-reaction force drawn from the resident infantry battalion at Basra Palace as part of Operation 'Armageddon' (the codename for Battle Group support to UKSF). Armageddon Platoon also provided mobility support for the SAS, giving the Regiment access to Warrior and later Bulldog armoured vehicles; and it would often escort the SAS strike teams to their objective, fighting the way through hostile neighbourhoods if necessary, maintaining a security cordon at the target while the SAS went to work, and then escorting them back out, often under heavy fire.

Hostage rescues

The Regiment also conducted a number of hostage rescues during its time in Iraq. Among these their two most high-profile missions were the rescues of a peace campaigner, Norman Kember, and of two of their own who had been snatched by Iraqi Police sympathetic to the insurgents.

Norman Kember was taken hostage in November 2005 somewhere in the Baghdad area, and Operation 'Lightwater' was launched to find and rescue him. He was released in March 2006 after an operation apparently involving the Regiment, the SFSG, and members of the Canadian Joint Task Force 2

An image of poor quality but considerable historical interest; it shows the then-commander of the American JSOC, LtGen Stanley McChrystal (second right), alongside the then-CO of 22 SAS, accompanying a Task Force Black assault team in Iraq. Of A Sqn's tour in 2007 Gen McChrystal said: 'I know one squadron that in a six-month rotation of 180 days, I think they did 175 operations. That's going out every night into combat. I got to go with them several times. These were not just drive-around patrols, these were combat assaults. Sometimes right in on the objective by air, more often land away and walk in several kilometres so that you could achieve some surprise'.

who were in Baghdad to assist in the search for two Canadians held with Kember (one of whom was executed by the insurgents). The operation was apparently based on intelligence from a captured insurgent who was subjected to tactical questioning by SAS operators. The insurgent phoned his colleagues to warn them to leave the hostages unharmed or face the wrath of the SAS. Not surprisingly, when the operators conducted a hasty house assault the hostage-takers were nowhere to be seen. Kember attracted significant criticism for his begrudging thanks to his rescuers. According to Mark Urban's *Task Force Black* (an indispensable read for all who wish to understand the SAS campaign in Iraq), no fewer than 50 targets had been raided looking for Kember, with the SAS conducting 44 of these and detaining 47 individuals. Intriguingly, only four of these targets were considered 'dry holes' of little or no intelligence value; these numbers speak volumes about the spidery connections between the insurgents, criminal gangs, and al Qaeda.

In September 2005 two members of A Sqn, conducting covert surveillance in Basra on a senior Iraqi Police officer suspected of working for the insurgents, were captured after a brief gunfight and chase by Iraqi Police. (Pictures broadcast on Iranian TV show the SAS operators to have been heavily armed, with a Minimi Para LMG and a 66mm LAW rocket in addition to their L119A1 carbines. Considering this firepower, they showed admirable restraint in not engaging the Iraqi policemen in a protracted firefight.) At the time the Iraqi Police in the south had been heavily infiltrated by Shia militias, and the two SAS men were in grave danger. Beaten and hooded, they were taken to the Jamiat Police Station, where they were interrogated.

A reinforced troop from A Sqn supported by a platoon from 1 Para (the battalion recently allocated as the core of the new SFSG) flew to Basra, while overhead the Americans and British deployed a number of UAVs and helicopters to maintain eyes-on the police station. The Americans even famously offered the use of a Delta squadron to break the SAS men out. With the SAS in the air, regular British forces surrounded the Jamiat Police Station and were themselves attacked by rioting mobs. The two captives were rushed out of the building into a waiting car, and driven away before the British could complete their cordon. Eventually British Warrior AFVs moved in and began to demolish the police station. At the same time, Task Force Black operators conducted an explosive entry on a suburban house to which a surveillance helicopter had tracked the two prisoners, who were recovered shaken but alive; evidently the hostage-takers, anticipating an SAS assault, had chosen discretion over valour. This incident led to Task Force Black being named in the media, so its title was changed to Task Force Knight.

In fact, the SAS 'spun up' for a regular stream of hostage-rescue missions as actionable intelligence was developed, including a number of operations targeting the kidnappers of five British security contractors and their charge, a consultant working with the Iraqi Finance Ministry. Sadly, they were never found; the security contractors were executed, although the consultant was finally released after several years.

Targeting the bombers

In 2006 the Regiment had been given a subset of high-value targets, namely the suicide-bomb network operating in and around Baghdad. This network used both suicide car bombs (known in the jargon as SVBIEDs or Suicide Vehicle-Borne IEDs), and fanatical or mentally ill people with bombs strapped to their bodies (including al Qaeda's infamous use of young people with Down's syndrome as suicide bombers). The relentless strike operations eventually paid dividends for the population of Baghdad and Coalition Forces operating in the capital; the numbers of suicide bomb attacks fell from a reported 150 a month to 2 a month over the period 2006–2007.

Lieutenant-General McChrystal of JSOC has been quoted praising the Regiment's contribution in Iraq, and specifically A Sqn's 2007 tour, in generous terms. General David Petraeus, in 2007 the Coalition commander in Iraq, also singled out the Regiment for public praise (to the dismay of the publicity-averse Director UKSF): 'They have helped immensely in the Baghdad area, in particular, to take down the al Qaeda car bomb networks and other al Qaeda operations… they have done a phenomenal job in that regard.' In Basra, however, as the British negotiated a settlement of sorts with the Shia militias in 2007, Task Force Spartan were withdrawn and SAS operations officially ended in southern Iraq.

Elsewhere the war against al Qaeda ground on, and the Coalition made major gains against the terrorists and the wider Sunni insurgency. The SAS maintained their demanding schedule, hitting multiple targets every night and gradually bleeding the insurgency dry by attrition of its leaders,

WEAPONS
(These images are to a common scale.)

1: Heckler & Koch HK53 assault rifle
The 5.56x45mm HK53 was a popular choice in Northern Ireland; it was scarcely larger than an MP5 (less than 24in long with the butt collapsed), but was chambered for the heavier rifle round, increasing both penetration through intervening cover and terminal effects on the target. It was largely replaced by the G3K firing the heavier 7.62x51mm round.

2: L119A1 carbine
The standard SAS individual weapon; this stencil-camouflaged example is fitted with an EO Tech optic, a PEQ-2 infra-red laser illuminator, a Tango Down vertical forward grip, and a suppressor.

3: L119A2 carbine
Announced in 2014, the L119A2 is the mid-life upgrade to the L119A1. Colt Canada are delivering each weapon with two upper receivers with differing barrel lengths, one for the carbine and one for the CQB version. This example shows an

improved VLTOR-style stock, folding back-up 'iron sights', a Picatinny rail along the top of the weapon and three sets of rails on the foregrip, and a PMAG magazine with round-counting window, along with a new suppressor-ready flash eliminator.

4: L119A1 CQB carbine
This 'shorty' Close-Quarter Battle version of the L119A1, with an ACOG optic, features a 10in barrel, better suited for room-clearing or for carrying in vehicles during surveillance operations.

5: Accuracy International AES sniper rifle
This integrally suppressed 7.62x51mm bolt-action weapon is fitted with a Schmidt & Bender optic and a folding bipod.

6: Accuracy International AWSM sniper rifle
The Arctic Warfare Super Magnum in .338 Lapua Magnum calibre, here with bipod extended and suppressor attached, was later adopted in modified form by the regular British Army as the L115 series.

This SAS operator wearing American DCUs is equipped for a night 'house assault' in Iraq; his kit is essentially similar to that shown on page 44, but there are subtle differences. His sand-colour helmet seems to have been hand-camouflaged with brown 'scribbles'. His L119A1 (also camouflage-painted) is attached to his armour by a single-point sling, ensuring that he retains his main weapon whatever happens. Note how comparatively little ammunition assaulters carried for these operations: this soldier has just three extra magazines for his carbine and two for his pistol. For speed of access and reloading the magazine pouches are worn open, and rubber Magpuls are fitted to the magazines. Pistol magazines are carried on the sides of the carbine magazine pouches; always carrying items in the same place aids 'muscle memory' when shooting under high duress, e.g. after being wounded, or disoriented by an explosion.

facilitators, bomb-makers and logistics providers. The Regiment could not maintain such an operational pace without casualties, however. In April 2007 and again in November 2007, RAF Puma helicopters crashed while supporting SAS operations; in each incident SAS operators were killed and a larger number seriously wounded. In Baghdad in September 2007 a veteran SAS sergeant was shot and killed during a house assault on a suicide-bomb cell.

Many have argued that the SAS and JSOC paved the way for the success of the so-called 'Iraq Surge' of 2007 and the 'Anbar Awakening' of Sunni tribes taking up arms against al Qaeda. In fact, a key to the latter initiative was the Strategic Engagement Cell led by Gen McChrystal's deputy, the former SAS officer and DSF, LtGen Graeme Lamb. Part of his strategy involved a 'carrot-and-stick' approach: he offered Sunni leaders a face-saving

One from a series of photos of operators of the SFSG's Task Force Maroon from 1 Para at the joint allied helipad in Baghdad, 2008. The paras wear desert-pattern DPM, and a mix of chest rigs worn over low-profile body armour, or Blackhawk assault vests. Note both 24 chest- and 12 sleeve-mounted loops for Hatton shotgun ammunition, and the breaching shotgun attached by bungee cord to the black vest at far right. The special 12-bore rounds fire single frangible projectiles made of metallic powder bonded with wax; at very close range they have enough kinetic energy to dismount locked doors, but they then disperse almost completely so as to reduce the threat to anybody beyond the door. On the left is the tail rotor of an Army Air Corps Lynx helicopter; a type often employed by SAS aerial sniper teams.

way to side with the Coalition against al Qaeda, accompanied by a thinly veiled threat that those who did not join in the reconciliation would be returned to JSOC and SAS target lists.

As operations finally began to wind down, B Sqn was assigned the final rotation as Task Force Knight. They made Regimental history with the first combat HALO jump of the Iraq campaign, but also suffered tragic losses. In Tikrit, four SAS operators were seriously wounded and one was killed along with their Combat Assault Dog when entering a target house. Eventually an AC-130H Spectre aerial gunship was vectored in to level the target houses, as the weight of insurgent fire had by then made any ground approach suicidal.

Operation 'Crichton', the UKSF contribution to Operation 'Telic' and more broadly to Operation 'Iraqi Freedom', ended in May 2009. Estimates of the SAS's impact point to a figure of about 3,000 insurgents and terrorists captured and perhaps 400 killed. The Regiment had lost five operators in house assaults, three in helicopter crashes, and dozens more wounded.

AFGHANISTAN, 2006–2014
Operation 'Kindle'
As noted above, the SBS had primacy in Afghanistan while the SAS fought the long war in Iraq. However, with the emergence of the Taliban insurgency British troops became involved in 'some of the most intense warfighting seen since Korea' after their deployment to Helmand Province in 2006. Typically, special operations were handled by a squadron of the SBS and SRR under Operation 'Kindle' (the Afghanistan equivalent to Operation 'Crichton' in Iraq), supported by an SFSG company, and known collectively as Task Force 42. After the Iraq drawdown in 2009, two SAS squadrons were dispatched to Afghanistan, and that country soon became the Regiment's focus.

Their return to Afghanistan occurred at the same time as Gen McChrystal took over as commander of the International Security and Assistance Force/ Afghanistan (ISAF), and in 2009 he instigated an 'Afghan Surge'. This aimed to knock the Taliban off-balance by means of a number of large-scale operations, often deep into their safe areas, to bring his COIN concept of

Members of B Sqn, 22 SAS in Afghanistan, c.2010. Both wear Paraclete SOHPC plate carriers over their Crye MultiCam uniforms, and carry their pistols in waist holsters. The B Sqn patch of a bear's paw-print (right) originated in tales of a bear mascot adopted by squadron members in Malaya.

'clear-hold-build' to fruition. Simply put, the idea was to clear a contested area of insurgents, place enough troops in that area to hold it, and finally to start building – both in terms of quick infrastructure reconstruction to get the population on side, and of installing a basic local government structure to combat the Taliban's 'shadow governors'. Special Operations Forces were key to this strategy; McChrystal planned a campaign to degrade Taliban leadership and facilitators similar to the one he had masterminded in Iraq. Indeed, the 'Afghan Surge' of 2009 resulted in the number of kill-or-capture missions more than tripling, as JSOC and UKSF shifted their focus and their 'industrial-strength' CT campaign to Afghanistan. Later that year, 'Iraq Surge' architect Gen David Petraeus replaced Gen McChrystal as commander of ISAF after the latter's resignation over media comments attributed to his staff. This change did not cause any decrease in the numbers of strike operations targeting the Taliban 'irreconcilables' who would never be tempted to the negotiating table.

High-value target interdiction

One leaked report of such an operation stated that 'TF 42 conducted Operation BEETHOVEN 5 against JPEL target BEETHOVEN, IS1473. BEETHOVEN and three other INS were killed'. This curt report masks what was in reality a dangerous capture-or-kill mission launched against a high-value insurgent target. BEETHOVEN was the codename of an individual important enough to have been listed on the Joint Prioritised Effects List – effectively a hit-list of high-value insurgent targets. The fact that this mission was numbered BEETHOVEN 5 indicates that the target had already escaped capture or death four times previously. The IS1473 notation is a geographical grid reference to the location of the operation, which was south of Lashkar Gah in Helmand Province. The summary of results indicates that the target and three other insurgents were killed by the UKSF operators. BEETHOVEN was in fact Mullah Ziauddin, who, according to a NATO press release, was 'a Taliban commander who was intimately involved in the procurement, construction and emplacement of IEDs'. The same press release characteristically makes no mention of UKSF involvement, referring to the strike element simply as 'ISAF forces'.

In 2011, the senior British officer in Afghanistan briefly lifted the cloak of secrecy surrounding SAS operations to confirm that the Regiment were 'taking out 130–140 mid-level Taliban leaders every month'. This was in

Members of the SFSG in Afghanistan during a long-range reconnaissance mission in 2010; the central man wears a SOHPC plate carrier over a UBACS shirt. The vehicles are Jackal 1 MWMIKs, developed from the Menacity SRV/OAV.

spite of significant changes in the operational dynamic from that in Iraq. The rules of engagement had changed, ostensibly placing Afghan security forces in the lead on all such operations, even though in reality they were largely planned, executed and supported by the Regiment. Political fallout around civilian casualties caused by what Afghans termed 'night raids' meant that the SAS would often have to use an interpreter to call out their targets on a megaphone before conducting entry. General McChrystal instituted a policy of 'courageous restraint' that he required all Coalition Forces to follow, making it increasingly difficult to authorize air strikes in populated areas.

Greater co-operation with allied SOF, and the inherited benefits derived

In a scene rather evocative of the old wartime Long Range Desert Group in North Africa, a UKSF patrol, probably from the SBS, is seen conducting an orders group during a halt in Afghanistan. The Menacity vehicle is heavily stowed for a long-range operation, and mounts both single and twin GPMGs. The operators display a wide range of uniforms, kit, and civilian outdoor gear; note too, on the ground at bottom centre, an AK47 assault rifle fitted with a Grip Pod bipod.

Regular British troops train within Camp Bastion, Helmand Province, in 2011, while an SAS Bushmaster PMV drives past in the background. This one is generally similar to the vehicle photographed in Iraq three years earlier (see page 40), but has additional bar armour to counter rocket-propelled grenades. The Bushmaster has a V-section bottom hull to deflect mine blast, a remote weapon station, and two rear top hatches which can be fitted with swing-out MG mounts; it can carry a two-man crew plus nine soldiers and their kit, and has a long range. (© PA, photo Owen Humphreys)

from the close collaboration with Gen McChrystal and Delta Force in Iraq, led to improved targeting. A respected US journalist and author, Linda Robinson, wrote of the hunt for a Taliban leader named Mullah Dadullah: "A [US] special mission unit had been sent... to help track Dadullah by tapping into the communications of his brother, who had been captured in Pakistan but later released. Upon learning that Mullah Dadullah was planning to re-enter Afghanistan, the special mission unit passed the tip to British special operations units in Helmand. The British commandos killed Dadullah after a fierce four-hour battle."

In the flat light of early morning or evening, a Menacity SRV/OAV provides overwatch for an RAF Chinook resupply somewhere in Afghanistan; the tactical logistics techniques of UKSF give their mobility elements long range and endurance. The twin-mounted GPMGs fitted to this vehicle are particularly favoured for their suppressive-fire capability.

The Regiment conducted all manner of 'high-value target interdiction operations' in Afghanistan, largely in support of British forces in Helmand. Operators from the SRR would typically conduct surveillance on the target in concert with UKSF ISTAR assets including mini-UAVs (drones). Once a solid picture of the target and his movements was developed, a target package would be passed to the SAS, and planning on how best to interdict the target would begin. This might result in a ground or helicopter assault force landing at a target location to attempt to seize the individual. If the threat to Coalition Forces was considered too great, and the target could be tracked to an area where collateral damage could be minimized, he might be taken out by deploying airborne snipers, or by a Hellfire missile fired from an RAF Reaper drone.

Hostage rescue

As in Iraq, UKSF were involved in a number of hostage rescues in Afghanistan. However, they were not involved in the attempted rescue of British aid worker Linda Norgrove on 8 October 2010, when she was inadvertently killed by a fragmentation grenade thrown by one of the rescue team from JSOC's SEAL Team Six. (Eastern Afghanistan was that SEAL team's familiar patch, and the SAS were apparently fully committed in the south at that time.)

The SAS did carry out a mission alongside the SEALs in June 2012, to rescue another British aid worker and her three Kenyan and Afghan colleagues who were being held in the far north-east of the country. Operation 'Jubilee' was launched when signals intercepts indicated that the hostages were in danger of being moved across the border into Pakistan. The hostages had been split into pairs and were being held in two separate caves; seven insurgents guarded one group, believed to be the two Afghans, while four more guarded the Kenyan and British aid workers. To reach the target location, a joint SAS/SEAL assault force landed several kilometres away by

A joint force element of SBS and SFSG in Afghanistan. The SFSG operators wear a mix of Osprey Mk 1 and ECBA body armour along with PLCE assault vests, suggesting that they are probably from the Group's Royal Marine Commando component. An Accuracy International AWSM sniper rifle sits on its bipod in the left foreground.

helicopter to preserve the element of surprise, and made a difficult night approach through surrounding forests. Both teams moved into their final assault positions in the pre-dawn gloom, and launched their assaults simultaneously. 'Flashbang' grenades blinded the guards, who were quickly shot and killed. None of the gunmen survived either the SAS or SEAL assaults, and all the hostages were rescued unharmed.

Village Stability Operations

For the first time in its recent history, the SAS also became involved in supporting the 'non-kinetic' COIN campaign in Afghanistan known as Village Stability Operations or VSOs. Although the Regiment are considered past masters of COIN, the overwhelming majority of SAS taskings since 2001 have been based on Direct Action. General McChrystal laid out his plan to win back the 'hearts and minds' of the Afghan people by using Coalition SOF to implement a wide-ranging village stability programme. Units like the SEALs and the SAS would be responsible for the development of 'security bubbles' around key villages that were threatened by Taliban influence. One US Special Forces officer noted the practical limitations of the kill-or-capture campaign when 'you were sending the SAS out after a third-tier local leader'. Inevitably, SOF would target ever lower-ranking insurgents as the higher-value targets were killed, captured, or fled across the border into Pakistan. At some point using the SAS on such lowly targets made little operational sense when their expertise could be better utilized elsewhere, as in the VSO programme.

NEW WARS

Just as in the second half of the 20th century, the SAS has been involved in numerous 'small wars' during the early part of the 21st century. The so-called 'Arab Spring' and the rise of numerous al Qaeda-inspired jihadist groups in Africa, along with the collapse of Syria and the threat of ISIL, have kept the Regiment busy.

These new conflicts have also seen a new element created within the UK Special Forces Group – E Squadron. The new squadron was apparently raised some time in 2007 as a joint UKSF unit to operate in denied areas of the globe, typically in close concert with or direct support of SIS operations. Intriguingly, the equally secretive 4 Sqn of the Australian SASR was established with a very similar role. An early mission to escort what were

assumed to be members of the SIS on a mission to meet with rebel leaders in Libya ended in the capture of both the SIS officers and their protection team by a rival anti-government faction. Apparently the protection element drawn from E Sqn only surrendered at the insistence of the SIS officers, who feared diplomatic consequences should the operators open fire. The personnel were repatriated, and a reinforced troop from D Sqn later deployed to Libya in civilian dress to mentor anti-Gaddafi rebels.

In Mali, UKSF have reportedly maintained a presence with SIS in support of French special operations as part of Operation 'Serval', although this seems to be an intelligence fusion-and-exchange cell rather than Direct Action. A small UKSF element was also reportedly operating in Yemen alongside JSOC units. It has been said that a small joint UKSF/SIS element operating with JSOC supported the December 2014 SEAL Team Six raid to rescue a British hostage, which tragically ended in his death and that of a South African fellow captive.

According to reports, some 200 UKSF personnel including an SAS squadron are deployed to northern Iraq as part of Operation 'Shader' against ISIL forces, operating in a number of civilian Land Rovers and Toyota Hilux pick-ups. A Kurdish Peshmerga general admitted that both US and UK SOF were supporting his troops: 'Their special forces don't take any part in the fighting. They are only taking a role in training and teaching, and also as observers. As observers they go to the front line, but don't do any fighting.' America's JSOC has established Task Force 27 based in northern Iraq with the express purpose of conducting Direct Action missions against high-value ISIL targets, and its operators were involved in several hostage-rescue and kill-or-capture missions into eastern Syria in 2014 and 2015. If the war against ISIL intensifies, there is little doubt that the Regiment will be back again alongside their Delta Force colleagues. According to some reports, an SAS team conducted a close target reconnaissance in eastern Syria prior to a Delta operation in May 2015.

A rather shadowy view of soldiers from the SFSG in Afghanistan, late 2008. Although equipped with Crye uniforms and Paraclete RAV plate carriers, they are armed with L85A2s rather than L119A1s, since there were then too few of the latter to arm the new SFSG and SRR. The photo also shows, under magnification, a suppressed HK417s with Schmidt & Bender optic carried by the unit marksman. Small numbers of optics-equipped G3Ks were apparently employed before larger stocks of HK417 became available.

In Afghanistan too, even after Operation 'Herrick XX' came to an end in December 2014, Operation 'Kindle' continues, with a reported squadron-strength presence of the SAS remaining to conduct strike operations. Earlier, the SFSG maintained a high operational tempo months after the official end of offensive operations by UK forces, as inadvertently confirmed in the Airborne Journal, *Pegasus*. An SFSG officer in 2013 mentioned his men operating alongside their partnered Afghan Interior Ministry Task Force 444 special operations unit 'killing the enemy in the close battle', targeting bomb-makers and logistics. Such operations in Afghanistan will most likely continue for the foreseeable future.

A common heritage

As noted above, all UKSF now come under the command of the Director Special Forces, a general officer. The Directorate was stood up in 1987 to act as something like a British version of the American Joint Special Operations Command. Its assets are 22 SAS, the SBS, the SRR, the SFSG, 18 (UKSF) Signal Regt, the Joint SF Aviation Wing, and E Squadron. As noted in the footnote on page 4, the Reserve units 21 and 23 SAS are no longer formally part of UK Special Forces.

Several of the newer additions to UKSF deserve brief explanation. The Special Forces Support Group, based on a rotating 1 Para company and a squadron each from the Royal Marine Commandos and RAF Regiment, was raised in 2005 to operate in close support of the SAS, SBS and SRR. They are roughly similar to the US Army Rangers in that they can conduct unilateral raids, but typically act as both blocking and quick-reaction forces for the so-called 'Tier 1' units. They also have a rotating company group trained in CT to support the on-call SAS and SBS CT squadrons.

In 2010, Australian SASR operator Ben Roberts Smith was awarded the Victoria Cross for valour beyond the call of duty in Afghanistan. Here he carries a borrowed 7.62x51mm Mk14 Mod 0 battle rifle, mounting both an EOTech optic and Aimpoint magnifier, on a bungee-cord sling. Note the national flag left-sleeve patch, and the 'dump pouch' at his hip. (Courtesy FCE MMT Sgt Paul Evans, Australian Defense Force)

The Special Reconnaissance Regiment (SRR) is another recent addition. With a heritage dating back to the Army Surveillance Unit and the 'Det' of Northern Ireland fame, the SRR was raised to provide specialist long-range reconnaissance, covert surveillance, and both human and technical intelligence-gathering for UK Special Forces. The SRR today conducts many of the battlefield surveillance tasks that were once the bread-and-butter of the SAS itself, including its elite Surveillance Reconnaissance Cell.

In a number of Commonwealth and allied countries, units with strong traditional links to 22 SAS remain. The Australian Special Air Service Regiment (SASR), founded in 1957, is perhaps the closest in structure to 22 SAS. To its original three numbered sabre squadrons, a fourth was apparently added in 2010 to provide a dedicated covert reconnaissance, surveillance and advanced-force operations capability to work alongside or detached to Australian intelligence agencies. The SASR has been heavily committed in Afghanistan since 2001, and provided a Special Forces Task Group that

A rare close-up shot of the UKSF individual carbine, the 5.56x45mm Diemaco/Colt Canada L119A1, with Trijicon ACOG optic and (visible under magnification) British markings. (Courtesy Kelly Stumpf, Colt Canada)

operated alongside the British SAS during the invasion of Iraq. SASR operators are today again deployed to Iraq as part of Operation 'Okra'. The SASR are based at Campbell Barracks in Perth, Western Australia, and provide an on-call CT presence (along with a similar East Coast-based capability from 2 Commando Regt), structured around the British SP Team concept. Two of Australia's four Victoria Cross recipients for service in Afghanistan were from the Special Air Service Regiment.

The New Zealand SAS Group can also trace a direct lineage to 22 SAS. It was established as an SAS squadron in 1955, and served alongside 22 SAS in Malaya and Borneo before deploying to Vietnam alongside the Australian SASR. It also served with the SASR and the SBS during the East Timor intervention that began in 1999. Today it is composed of two SAS sabre squadrons, a Commando CT squadron and an EOD squadron. The SAS squadrons have operated extensively in Afghanistan as Task Force 81, losing several members in action and receiving an award of the Victoria Cross before the NZSAS mission officially ended in March 2012.

Two European units can also claim descent from the original World War II Special Air Service. The 1st Parachute Bn of the Belgian Paracommando Regt continued the lineage of the wartime Belgian 5th SAS until 2010, when it was subsumed into the newly raised Army Special Forces Group; the unit maintain their metal SAS cap badge and motto. The traditions of the wartime French 3rd and 4th SAS are also maintained by 1st Marine Infantry Parachute Regt (1er Régiment de Parachutistes d'Infanterie de Marine, 1er RPIMa), whose breast badge incorporates 'SAS' and *'Qui Ose Gagne'* ('Who Dares Wins'). The 1er RPIMa is organized along SAS lines, with each company (roughly equivalent to a squadron) specializing in a method of insertion or specialist skills (HALO and HAHO parachuting, small boat and SCUBA, mobility, and mountaineering and Arctic warfare). The unit has seen extensive action in Afghanistan, Central Africa, and Operation 'Serval' in Mali.

OPPOSITE

A member of the SFSG caught by the camera as he disembarks from a US Marine Corps CH-53 after a joint operation with the US Marines in Helmand in 2013. He wears Crye MultiCam uniform and commercial hiking boots, and his weapon is the 7.62x51mm HK417 adopted by UKSF as a marksman rifle. (Courtesy Sgt Gabriela Garcia, US Marine Corps)

WEAPONS

The legendary 9x19mm L9A1 Browning pistol was officially replaced in the SAS by the SIG-Sauer L105A1 or P226 in the late 1980s, ending a close

An SAS soldier trains with a sound-suppressed Heckler & Koch MP5SD3 sub-machine gun somewhere in Iraq.

relationship with the venerable Browning Hi-Power that stretched back to the Regiment's wartime origins. SAS P226s are routinely equipped with a rail-mounted weapon light and an extended 20-round magazine; the smaller P228 is also carried when concealability is a key requirement. Recently the 9x19mm Glock has been increasingly employed by the Regiment in a number of variants, including the compact Glock 19.

The Heckler & Koch MP5 family of 9x19mm sub-machine guns, once synonymous with the SAS, are rarely employed today. The 'Hockler' is reserved for hostage rescues in domestic or permissive environments, since frangible 9x19mm rounds are less prone to ricochet or over-penetrate. For hostage rescues in Afghanistan, however, the CQB version of the standard 5.56x45mm L119A1 carbine is used, as it can engage targets at ranges far beyond the capacity of the MP5.

In Northern Ireland the SAS used a range of 9x19mm MP5s, 5.56x45mm HK53s and (later) 7.62x51mm G3Ks, as well as Remington shotguns, the latter loaded with Hatton breaching rounds to defeat locked doors. Before the G3K was developed at the request of the Regiment a number of captured Argentine-issue FN FALs with side-folding stocks were procured.

During Operation 'Granby' the Regiment's patrols carried 5.56x45mm M16s equipped with 40mm M203 underslung grenade-launchers, and 5.56x45mm Minimi light machine guns. SAS personnel deployed to the

---

H **WEAPONS & INSIGNIA**

1: Remington 870 shotgun

One of the Regiment's roles in Northern Ireland was to provide an immediate hostage-rescue capability should a British soldier be captured. This 12-bore Remington 870 shotgun features a folding stock, and would probably have been loaded with Hatton breaching rounds to defeat door locks and hinges.

2: Heckler & Koch MP5K sub-machine gun

Despite its limited penetration, at less than 13in long the 9x19mm MP5K sub-machine gun was popular among UKSF in Northern Ireland. Note the magazine clamp holding a second 30-round magazine alongside the first.

3: L74A1 shotgun

A hand-camouflaged example of the 12-bore L74A1 shotgun as modified for Afghanistan by UK Special Forces. It features a collapsible buttstock, a Tango Down foregrip, an Aimpoint Micro optic, a PEQ-15 laser illuminator (on the right side), and in this case what appears to be an improvised sling.

Insignia:

4: Special Air Service badge worn on the sand-colour beret, with the 'Who Dares Wins' motto on the scroll. The badge of the Regiment is not in fact a 'winged dagger', although that term has entered into common use even amongst Special Forces. It is in fact a representation of King Arthur's sword, Excalibur, surrounded by flames.

5: Special Boat Service badge worn on the Royal Marine Commando green beret, with Excalibur rising from the waves and the 'By Strength and Guile' motto of the SBS.

6: Special Reconnaissance Regiment badge worn on the khaki beret common to most British Army infantry units. It shows Excalibur and a Corinthian helmet, with 'Reconnaissance' on the scroll.

7: Special Forces Support Group drop-zone flash – a lightning bolt superimposed on a downwards-pointing Excalibur – as worn on the right sleeve. SFSG operators wear the beret and cap badge of their parent units.

1

2

4

3

5

6

7

In the dimly lit interior of a Task Force Knight objective in Iraq, 2007, an operator can be seen carrying not only a suppressed carbine but also, secured under his left arm, an L74A1 sawn-off shotgun with spare shells in 'Side Saddle' loops.

Balkans with the standard-issue L85A1 (SA80) to support their cover as UN personnel. Operation 'Barras' saw a mix of M16s and newer Canadian Diemaco rifles and carbines carried, along with the Minimi and GPMG.

In 2000, selection trials were held for a new SAS individual weapon, and three contenders were tested to their limits: the Heckler & Koch G36, the SIG SG551, and the Diemaco C8SFW. The weapon submitted by Diemaco (now Colt Canada) won, and a modified C8SFW was adopted as the L119A1 Special Forces Individual Weapon. The standard version, officially designated as an assault rifle, has a 15.7in barrel, whilst the weapon's upper receiver can be replaced with the 10in carbine or CQB barrel for an even smaller platform. The L119A1 has been supplemented in recent years by the Special Forces Ultra Compact Individual Weapon (UCIW); with an even shorter (8in) barrel and measuring only 22in overall, this still fires the 5.56x45mm round. The UCIW has been deployed operationally in Afghanistan, being carried by those whose primary role is not as assaulters – such as breachers, dog-handlers and medics. The L119A1 was itself upgraded in 2013 to the new L119A2 standard.

SAS snipers have used a wide range of rifles including the 7.62x51mm Heckler & Koch PSG-1 and the .22-250 Tikka M55, but the most common platform has been the Accuracy International; indeed, the SBS and SAS were the company's first military customers, with the Regiment purchasing 32 of AI's 7.62x51mm Precision Magazine (PM) variant in 1985. Today the Regiment has largely settled on the heavier .338 Lapua Magnum ammunition, and after using the AI Arctic Warfare Super Magnum in this calibre for many years in Iraq and Afghanistan, the unit has switched to a Canadian design called the PGW Timberwolf. The SAS has also deployed the 7.62x51mm Heckler & Koch 417 as a marksman rifle to support assaults, and the .50cal AW50 and Barrett M82A1 anti-matériel rifles.

Also synonymous with the Regiment is the 'flashbang' or 'stun' grenade. Developed originally as a diversionary device based on the older Thunderflash, scientists at Porton Down made an improved version that combined the loud report with a magnesium-based flash, deafening and blinding targets for up to five vital seconds. This G60 model was first used operationally in Mogadishu in October 1977 in support of GSG9. Today's versions, such as the Rheinmetall Mk13 BTV-EL used by the SAS, are vastly improved and non-pyrotechnic ('flashbangs' were blamed for starting at least one of the fires at the Iranian Embassy in 1980).

SELECT BIBLIOGRAPHY

Asher, Michael, *The Real Bravo Two Zero: The Truth Behind Bravo Two Zero* (London; Cassell & Co, 2002)

Asher, Michael, *The Regiment: The Real Story of the SAS* (London; Penguin Books, 2008)

Atkinson, Rick, *Crusade: The Untold Story of the Persian Gulf War* (New York; Houghton Mifflin, 1993)

Coburn, Mike, *Soldier Five: The Real Truth About The Bravo Two Zero Mission* (London, Mainstream Publishing, 2004)

Collins, Colonel Tim, *Rules of Engagement: A Life in Conflict* (London; Headline, 2006)

Connor, Ken, *Ghost Force: The Secret History of the SAS* (London; Cassell & Co, 1998)

Crossland, Peter 'Yorky', *Victor Two: Inside Iraq: the Crucial SAS Mission* (London; Bloomsbury Publishing, 1997)

Curtis, Mike, *CQB: Close Quarter Battle* (London; Corgi, 1998)

Dorman, Dr Andrew M, *Blair's Successful War: British Military Intervention in Sierra Leone* (Surrey; Ashgate Publishing, 2009)

Firmin, Rusty, *The Regiment: 15 Years in the SAS* (Oxford; Osprey, 2015)

Fowler, Will, *Certain Death In Sierra Leone: The SAS and Operation Barras 2000*, Raid 10 (Oxford; Osprey, 2010)

Geraghty, Tony, *This is the SAS: A pictorial history of the Special Air Service Regiment* (London; Fontana/Collins, 1983)

Geraghty, Tony, *Who Dares Wins: The Special Air Service –1950 to the Gulf War* (London; Abacus, 2002)

Harnden, Toby, *Bandit Country: The IRA and South Armagh* (London; Coronet Books, 2000)

Jennings, Christian, *Midnight In Some Burning Town: British Special Forces Operations from Belgrade to Baghdad* (London; Weidenfeld & Nicolson, 2004)

Lewis, Damien, *Operation Certain Death: the inside story of the SAS's greatest battle* (London; Century, 2004)

Lewis, Damien, *Zero Six Bravo: 60 Special Forces. 100,000 Enemy. The Explosive True Story.* (London; Quercus, 2013)

Nicol, Mark, *Ultimate Risk* (London; Macmillan, 2003)

Ratcliffe, Peter, DCM, *Eye Of The Storm: Twenty-five Years In Action With The SAS* (London; Michael O'Mara Books, 2000)

Robinson, Linda, *One Hundred Victories: Special Ops and the Future of American Warfare* (Philadelphia; Public Affairs, 2013)

Spence, Cameron, *All Necessary Measures* (London; Penguin, 1999)

Spence, Cameron, *Sabre Squadron* (London; Penguin, 1998)

Taylor, Peter, *Brits: The War against the IRA* (London; Bloomsbury Publishing, 2001)

Urban, Mark, *Big Boys Rules: The SAS and the Secret Struggle against the IRA* (London; Faber & Faber, 1992)

Urban, Mark, *Task Force Black: The Explosive True Story of the SAS and the Secret War in Iraq* (London; Little Brown, 2010)

Urban, Mark, *UK Eyes Alpha* (London; Faber & Faber, 1996)

Walker, Greg, *At The Hurricane's Eye: US Special Operations Forces from Vietnam to Desert Storm* (New York; Ivy Book, 1994)

INDEX